Weddings

A Complete Guide to All Religious and Interfaith Marriage Services

Weddings
A Complete Guide to
All Religious and Interfaith
Marriage Services
is a part of
The Life-Cycle Bookshelf
edited by
Yehiel Hayon

Alpha Publishing Company
is a division of
Special Edition, Inc.
Columbus, Ohio

Weddings

A Complete Guide to All Religious and Interfaith Marriage Services

By
Abraham J. Klausner

Alpha Publishing Company
Columbus, Ohio
1986

Copyright © 1986 by Abraham J. Klausner.

Library of Congress Cataloging in Publication Data

Klausner, Abraham J.
  Weddings: A Complete Guide to All Religious and Interfaith
  Marriage Services.
  (The Life-Cycle Bookshelf)
  1. Marriage service. 2. Weddings. I. Title. II. Series.
  BL619.M37K55   1986   392'.5   86-7892

ISBN 0-933771-00-2

Book design: Special Edition, Inc.
Cover design: Marty Husted

Contents

The camp at Allach was down the road from the Dachau concentration camp. I entered through the desolate gates and moved toward the large central building. Inside, an ominous silence pervaded the rows of cots, where each concentration camp victim struggled to embrace life now that liberation had come. At the far end of the room, a figure stood, outlined by rays of sunlight stretching down from the skylight above. This was my first encounter with Captain Sidney B. Burke, M.D. From that moment, we were bound by a determination to bring life and support to the survivors. This bond continued after our work was done until the hour of Sid's death, and beyond—for it was his bequest that makes this work possible.

Introduction

Prominent among social and religious changes presently influencing our lives is our attitude toward marriage and the manner in which it is solemnized. Societies, generally, have sought to contain marriages within their respective cultures. To that end, they have established rules and devised practices to discourage "strangers" from disrupting the comfort and security of familiar traditions. Currently such societies are falling apart. The universal ethic "Have we not all one Father, has not one God created us?" has taken hold in these concluding decades of the twentieth century.

Young people are less bound to a particular tradition and are more reluctant to submit to the exclusive aspects of its rules and practices. This is clearly manifest in the increasing number of mixed and ecumenical marriages, in which personal feelings and ambitions override social and religious expectations. This development has provoked discord and controversy in religious disciplines intent upon preserving the folkways of a people. In some disciplines there is total rejection of one who would contravene established theologies and practices. In others there is an appreciation of the cultural forces at work and a desire to lend the compassion of a tradition to those intent upon a marriage beyond expectations and restrictions of race and creed.

This dramatic change has necessitated new approaches to the marriage service in which the blessings of, at times, competitive religious theologies are invoked. This volume deals with the question of the mixed and ecumenical marriage and offers services for them as they are presently being developed.

Change in attitude toward marriage and the wedding service is multifaceted. We are witnessing not only an increasing tendency to

1

break with the exclusivity of tradition, but also a growing demand for the wedding service to reflect properly the thinking of a universal generation. For example, common to various services are the phrases "As long as we shall live" or "What God has put together, let no man put asunder." The implied concept, "marriage lasts forever," is popularly rejected and the sentiment "As long as we shall love" substituted. The practice of asking the question, "Who gives this woman away?" and concluding with the pronouncement, "You are now man and wife" is similarly rejected. Some feel these phrases attest to the inequality of male and female roles. In this volume the language of traditional services is considered and alternatives are recommended to respond to the wishes of the universal generation.

For centuries it was assumed that the responsibility for planning and presenting a wedding celebration rested with the bride's family. This custom derives from marriage agreements and contracts essential to the social and economic realities of ancient, closed societies. The traditional imposition of the groom's name upon the bride is rooted in antiquated social structures as well. In both cases serious changes are taking place today. This volume reviews cultural conditions that made for practices now subject to revision.

Finally, the reader will discover a variety of religious services, both traditional and innovative. This volume is intended as a guide for those planning a service reflective of their distinctive needs and convictions.

Weddings— For Everyone

I could, and perhaps should, introduce this section on the planning of a wedding, its ceremonies and celebrations, with a poetic outburst relating the joy, excitement, and expectations of marriage. My purpose, however, is to discuss and elaborate upon the details and problems often encountered in the planning stages for a wedding that can lend to the excitement of the hour, but often bruise the evolving drama. There is an inescapable bureaucratic side to wedding plans, the particulars of which are not always understood and rarely appreciated. I shall describe and offer helpful and relevant commentary on pertinent details, emphasizing variations that abound.

A WEDDING IS NOT A MARRIAGE

A distinction should be made between a wedding and a marriage. A marriage is a commitment, compelled by a host of feelings, represented by the catchall word "love." A marriage takes place when one person says to another, "I love you, I want you, I need you," and there is a reciprocity of feeling and expression. The wedding is a formal announcement and dramatization of this bond. Family and friends are invited to receive the news, witness, and celebrate the union. In early American towns and villages, banns for marriage were posted in the Square informing citizens of the impending union of two people.

A WEDDING IS A TENSE EXPERIENCE

Planning for a wedding is a tense experience for everyone involved: bride, groom, and their families. A minor detail, such as the selec-

3

tion, style, and color of a garment, may become a family battle-ground. A wedding represents significant judgments made by bride and groom. The expressed reactions of loved ones to the details of wedding plans are often heard as critical commentary concerning these private judgments. Therefore, those involved in making and assisting the couple with decisions pertaining to the wedding service, ceremony, or celebration are cautioned, if and when discontentment flares, to reflect upon their own anxieties as they may be prompted by the decision for marriage.

GIVEN IN MARRIAGE

Traditionally, it is said, "a child is *given* in marriage." The officiating minister pauses during the service to inquire, "Who gives this woman to this man?" In response, a father steps forward and says, "I give this woman to this man!" Some people feel this practice suggests an attitudinal inequity pertaining to the roles of men and women in marriage. Nevertheless, others focus upon the conviction, generally cherished, that parents do give children in marriage. The wedding ceremony is their formal expression of consent. Children often neither sense nor fully appreciate the emotional impact of the marriage of a child upon parents. Culturally, the marriage of a child represents the culmination of the parents' anxieties, fears, hopes, and expectations. To marry off a child with the confidence that it is well done, in the presence of people important to parents, gives substance to the parental role.

THE GUEST LIST

The guest list often brings out conflicting emotions in both parents and children. The list will, very likely, contain the names of family, friends, social and business acquaintances of parents. Parents celebrate with relatives and friends the full experience of having reared a child, and, in the words of Hebrew tradition, "brought the child, happily, to the wedding canopy." Bride and groom, with varying degrees of intensity, may fault the list, saying, "These are not our friends," implying that it is their wedding, and, first and foremost, their friends should be among the guests. It is only reasonable and right for the bride and groom to have their friends with them sharing in the "holy convocation" of their marriage. In this, as in other aspects of the wedding plans, an understanding and appreciation of the wants and needs of all involved will encourage proper decisions.

THE WEDDING GUESTS— WHAT ARE THEIR EXPECTATIONS?

A wedding is a "reaching out" experience. Guests are invited to witness the marriage. They constitute the select community in which the marriage is pronounced. The formal or public service and its celebration is also for them. It is not only proper, but imperative, that the feelings and sensitivities of the guests be considered in planning the wedding.

Bride and groom will remain oblivious to much of the detail during the wedding service and celebration. Between time spent in the receiving line and with the photographer, they will miss a substantial portion of the reception hour—unlike Uncle William, who will not only remember that the livers were cold, but will add, "The family knows I don't like liver!" The planning is best served when the concerns and expectations of the guests are carefully and sympathetically considered, even to the point of having special dishes prepared for those who, for diet or other reasons, require them.

During the planning stages, when deliberating the inclusion or exclusion of a symbol or folk practice in the wedding ceremony, the couple should consider the question, "Who will be present among our guests and what are their expectations?" This frequently makes choices and decisions easier to come by.

EARLY SCHEDULING CONSIDERATIONS

Before time and place are established, bride and groom should meet with their clergyperson to inform him/her of their plans and invite his/her participation. If the time and place have been previously established, the family minister may have to excuse himself/herself because of a previous commitment. The search for an officiant becomes distasteful, especially if one after another rejects the invitation. Bride and groom are often incensed by these rejections. In the belief that "all the world should love a lover," they feel their interests should be paramount. It is therefore recommended that families

5

should not enter into contractual agreements for the use of a facility, hotel, or catering establishment until the time and place have been communicated to and accepted by the minister.

THE WEDDING DAY

The day selected for a wedding should be considered in the light of general community practices. A day traditionally reserved for religious festivals and family gatherings should be avoided. A wedding planned for such a time would compel guests to choose between a family gathering and a wedding, thus disturbing well-established tradition.

Prohibited Days

Religious calendars specify days upon which marriages are not to be consummated. (For particulars pertaining to these practices, see chapters on individual religious and cultural traditions.) Though bride and groom may not feel bound or responsive to such a tradition, they should ask themselves, "How will our families and guests feel if we schedule our wedding for one of these days?" Remember, the guests consitute the community in which the wedding is received and welcomed.

The Menstrual Cycle

In some societies, the day for a wedding is selected in accordance with the bride's menstrual cycle. Although contemporary practices concerning the bride's menses is not ordinarily considered, the ancient practice might well be observed in scheduling a wedding. It is anticipated that the wedding day will include the sexual consummation of the marriage promise, an exciting and binding conjugal experience that should be properly planned for.

THE TIME FOR THE WEDDING

There are no formal restrictions for scheduling a time for a wedding. There are customs, however, that suggest that one time is better than another. In the Catholic faith, a wedding does not take place in the evening. Some say a wedding should take place on the upward swing of the clock. Obviously, the time selected will have some relationship to the kind of reception desired. A morning wedding may be followed by a breakfast or brunch, a noon wedding by a luncheon, an afternoon wedding by a reception, and an evening wedding by a dinner.

A question often raised when an invitation is issued, verbally or in print, is whether the actual time of the ceremony should be indicated or a time thirty minutes or so prior to the actual commencement of the ceremony. The custom is to anticipate the time of the ceremony by thirty minutes. This allows late-comers an "on-time" arrival. However, people have come to assume that no wedding starts on time and thus, stragglers invariably remain. If the invitation indicates the precise time of service, word, in one way or another, should be passed that the ceremony will begin at the time noted. Some append the word "prompt" to the time indicated on the invitation.

THE PLACE FOR THE WEDDING

Considerable thought should be given to choosing a place for the wedding service. From tradition to tradition, the service is considered variously: as *Kiddushin,* which means "sanctification," implying "a setting apart for a special purpose," as a "sacrament," and as a "religious service." All faiths are joined in a concept of marriage as touching upon the "holy." The place and the setting for the wedding, therefore, should be in keeping with the meaning and purpose of the service.

The Sanctuary
Most responsive and attractive is a sanctuary, a place where the symbols and the mystery of prayer attend upon the service. Unlike the silence of commercial, anonymous places, the very atmosphere of the sanctuary is alive, speaking the thoughts and wishes of all who have prayed within its walls.

Those planning a wedding often hesitate, especially when the guests are few in number, to opt for a sanctuary wedding, saying "The sanctuary is large, and we are few; we will be lost in the sanctuary." There should be no hesitancy to plan for a sanctuary wedding. The size of the room does not bear upon the service. One person, in prayer, in the largest sanctuary, fills the room. A wedding, even if limited to bride, groom, and their witnesses, properly and effectively takes place in a sanctuary.

7

The Home

A home, referred to in literature as a "small sanctuary," is an appropriate setting for a wedding. When a home wedding is planned, a place should be designated for the service. It might be marked off from the general area with an altar, canopy, or bower of flowers. A table should be provided to serve either as an altar before which bride and groom stand, or simply as a receptacle, on which the symbols of the service are placed.

A home wedding tends to the informal. The guests may be seated without altering the organization of the room or chairs may be arranged allowing for an aisle for the wedding party. Depending upon the number of guests, they may simply stand gathered about bride and groom.

The Garden Wedding

During summer months, garden weddings abound. The setting is beautiful and sacred. However, there are problems associated with a garden wedding. There is the problem of weather; not only rain, but wind and excessive heat. An alternate plan should be readily available if the weather proves disappointing.

If at all possible, a shaded area should be selected for the service. At one garden wedding, the guests refused to take their seats until the very last moment. Instead, they congregated in small patches of shade, reluctant to venture forth into the blazing sun beating down upon the chairs awaiting them. Even after the procession began, some stayed back, hugging the shade. It was just too hot for a garden wedding.

Sound may be another problem. An extremely attractive service took place on a small island reached by way of a picturesque bridge. Guests seated beyond the moat kept nudging one another inquiring as to what was being said. The voices did not carry. A sound system might have remedied the situation. A chair arrangement can help. Instead of placing chairs in a square formation reaching as far back as needed, they can be arranged in a semicircle, making each row as long as possible, curving to the sides of the area. In this way, the guests are kept close to bride and groom and not only hear the reading of the service, but also feel closer to the event.

Distracting traffic, vehicular or other, is another problem encountered in garden weddings. At one of the Hilton hotels, a wedding took place in a garden alongside the swimming pool. Hotel guests frolicked to the words of the service—providing an unwelcomed counterpoint to the service.

CLERGY OR LAYPERSON OFFICIANT

Clergypersons are not required to conduct a wedding service. A layperson can perform a service, with minimum participation by an authorized official as may be required by law. In some traditions a selected layperson, or dignitary, is routinely asked to read the service. The laws of some states provide for laypersons designated by a congregation the privilege of conducting a marriage service.

Justices of the courts are also empowered to conduct wedding services, though they are not generally required to do so. There are, however, territorial limits to their services in individual states. Justices of the Peace may officiate in their towns; County Court judges, in their counties; Civil, Criminal, and Family Court judges, in their cites; and Justices of the State Supreme Court, anywhere in the state.

WEDDING SERVICE FOR COUPLES LIVING TOGETHER BEFORE MARRIAGE

An increasing number of couples live together before marriage. Cohabitation out of wedlock is, if not sinful, unacceptable in most religions. Under such circumstances, a request for a wedding service may pose a problem. Various dioceses of the Catholic Church have placed special restrictions upon a wedding service for cohabitating couples. In St. Cloud, Minnesota, the Bishop has instituted a policy that such couples must live apart for three months before a priest will officiate at their marriage. In Bismarck, North Dakota, marriages involving such couples are performed privately only.

THE MARRIAGE LICENSE

A marriage is authorized by the state. Individual states vary in their requirements. A minimum age is established for a marriage that does not require parental consent. Most states require a blood test and a waiting period between the presentation of the blood test results and the issuance of a marriage license. This license is dated. It indicates the time span in which the wedding can take place. When, in an emergency, a wedding must take place prior to the time stipulated, a waiver can be obtained through the courts. The waiver, together with the license, is delivered to the officiating clergyperson.

9

From State to State

A clergyperson is authorized to perform a wedding service by the state in which he/she resides. Except for states with reciprocal arrangements (New York and Connecticut), individual states generally establish procedures for the performance of a service by out-of-state clergy. Massachusetts, for example, requires that the clergy apply to the Secretary of State and await authorization before conducting a service. Kentucky bars all out-of-state clergy from performing a wedding service. If a couple is intent upon inviting the services of an out-of-state clergyperson (usually one with whom they or their families have been associated), they should contact state authorities regarding requirements and procedures.

A Second License

When a wedding is repeated—a couple may be married in one state and wish to repeat the service for family and friends in another state —a second, or new, license is required. The certificate obtained from the officiant at the first service is not sufficient. Should the second service take place within the same state, the officiant is still required to request a state authorization for the wedding. When obtaining a marriage license, a request can be made for a second copy. This should be the case when there is both a civil and a religious service. One copy will be marked "For Religious Service."

Certificate of Marriage

It is general practice for a clergyperson to present a marriage certificate to the couple. Though not a legal document, the certificate confirms the fact of marriage. It is generally accepted by authorities such as the United States Passport Office for changing the status of the couple and issuing proper papers.

Jewish practice may involve a marriage *Ketubah,* a traditional and historic document, often artistically rendered. The particulars of the *Ketubah* are noted in the chapter on the Jewish wedding.

Witnesses to a Marriage

The laws of the various states require that a marriage be witnessed. The marriage license provides for the signature of witnesses. This document is usually signed before the wedding takes place.

A witness may be any individual of legal age. However, since the signing of the document is part of the drama of the wedding, photographers usually insist upon capturing the moment. Bride and groom should give some thought to the selection of their witnesses. The witnesses to the license may also be asked to sign a wedding certificate provided by the officiant. If bride and groom prefer, they may select a second set of witnesses for the marriage certificate, thus involving two more loved ones in the drama of the hour.

Wedding Without a License

Occasionally a clergyperson is asked to perform a wedding with the stipulation that no license will be forthcoming. The reasons may be as diverse as the cases. One couple explained, "We don't care to have the state a party to our marriage." Another older couple stated: "We are both on Social Security. Should we obtain a license, we will be deprived of income we cannot afford to lose. Yet we want our relationship known and sanctified, especially out of respect for our children."

The necessity of a license has been argued before legal authorities. In general, it has been ruled that a marriage performed in the absence of a license is valid and binding, but the officiating clergyperson or official has acted illegally and is subject to the implications of the law.

Medical Considerations

When applying for a license, as previously noted, most states require a blood test. The results are presented to the license office. This Wasserman test is for syphilis. In addition, it is imperative—though not required by the state—that bride and groom be tested for presence of Rh factor and genetic diseases. Tragedies occur when children are born to parents who are carriers of one of the genetically transmitted diseases, such as Tay-Sachs syndrome, sickle cell anemia, or hemophilia. Couples are advised to undergo complete physical examinations prior to marriage and, particularly if any irregularity is uncovered, to exchange the results of the examinations in the presence of their respective doctors.

If either bride or groom has undergone psychotherapy in recent years prior to the wedding, arrangements should be made for a session with the therapist. The importance of such an action cannot be overstated. To fail to do so would, in effect, preserve a "secret" which might, in time, insinuate itself upon the marriage, as did the serpent in the Garden of Eden, turning spouse, suspiciously, against spouse.

11

THE WEDDING INVITATION

The formal invitation, traditionally issued by the bride's family, is no longer a standard form. The forms included in this section reflect the changes taking place in family structures and attitudes toward the wedding ceremony in general.

The Formal Invitation

Mr. and Mrs. Joseph Newton
request the honour of your presence
at the marriage of their daughter
Gail Ruth
to
Richard Denver
on Thursday the eighteenth of December
nineteen hundred and eighty-one
at half after three o'clock
Temple Emanuel
Clearview Drive
Cheyenne, Wyoming

A combined family involvement in the planning and presentation of the wedding is becoming more common:

Mr. and Mrs. Joseph Newton
and
Mr. and Mrs. Jeremiah Denver
request the honour of your presence
at the marriage of their children
Gail and Richard
...

There are as many approaches to the wedding invitation as there are to the ceremony itself. Thus, an invitation may read:

Come and rejoice with us
at the marriage
of our daughter Gail Ruth
to Richard Denver
...

Invitations may require revision due to circumstances such as divorce and remarriage. The form used will in many cases depend upon the spirit that prevails in the respective families. The following variations indicate how an invitation can be written to suit every conceivable situation.

A Widow

Mrs. Joseph Newton
requests the honour of your presence
at the marriage of her daughter
Gail Ruth

...

A Divorced Mother

Mrs. Sarah Newton
requests the honour of your presence

- ...

Remarried Divorced Mother and New Husband

Mr. and Mrs. Henry Newton
request the honour of your presence
at the marriage of her *daughter*
Gail Ruth

...

or:

Mrs. Sarah Newton
is joined by her husband
Mr. Henry Newton
in requesting the honour of your presence
at the marriage of her daughter
Gail Ruth

...

or:

...
at the marriage of their beloved
Gail Ruth

13

Remarried Divorced Mother and Natural Father

Mr. Henry Williams
and
Mrs. David L. Jones
request the honour of your presence
at the marriage of their daughter
Gail Ruth

...

Divorced Parents

Mrs. Sara Perkins Williams
and
Mr. Henry Williams
request the honour of your presence
at the marriage of their daughter
Gail Ruth

...

The name of the parent with whom the daughter has been living prior to the wedding should appear first.

Groom's Family

Mr. and Mrs. Jeremiah Denver
request the honour of your presence
at the marriage of
Miss Gail Newton
to their son
Mr. Richard Denver

...

Bride and Groom

Miss Ellen Lloyd Prichard
and
Mr. Gareth Ellis Edwards
request the honour of your presence
at their marriage

...

14

THE CEREMONY

There is no right or proper wedding ceremony. The guiding principle in the planning of a wedding is the shared tradition or expectations of those concerned. People treasure an "image" of a wedding. They remember the feeling it evoked and meaning it conveyed at a previous time, and anticipate its repetition.

Wedding ceremonies fall into a number of patterns. In the planning of a wedding, elements of these patterns may be interchanged or selected at will. Innovations may enrich the experience.

The Formal American Wedding

The most familiar wedding, the one usually depicted on screen and stage, is the formal American wedding. It takes place in a sanctuary. The procession is in two parts. The first involves grandparents and parents. Once the guests have been seated by the ushers and the service is to begin, grandparents enter in pairs. When there is only one grandparent, she or he is ushered to a seat. This usher should be a close relation to the grandparent, either a child or a grandchild, though there is no restriction as to who should or should not escort a grandparent. Often one of the designated ushers, a friend of the bride or groom, is asked to serve as an usher for a grandparent.

Parents follow grandparents. They may proceed in pairs. However, when a bride is escorted by her father, the mother of the bride may be escorted by a child, a brother, or someone dear to her. The husband may wish to escort his wife. If he chooses to do so, he will escort his wife to her seat, then return to escort his daughter.

Those following grandparents and parents constitute the second part of the processional, or the "wedding party." It may consist of ushers, bridesmaids, maid or matron of honor, flower girl, ring bearer, bride, and her escort. The groom and the best man, together with the officiant, form their own company and appear in their respective places at the altar without pomp or ceremony.

The minister, best man, and groom fill their respective places. The groom stands forward, the best man to one side. The wedding party proceeds, either as a company moving together, properly spaced, or one at a time. The ushers take their places; bridesmaids follow. Ushers and bridesmaids may be interlaced or may proceed in pairs, forming an honor guard. Next, the matron of honor proceeds to a des-

15

ignated place to attend the bride, followed by the bridesmaid who stands in company with the matron of honor. If there is no matron of honor, the bridesmaid stands alone to one side of the bride. The ring bearer takes his place between the best man and the officiant; the flower girl stands between the maid of honor and the officiant. Last, the bride enters with her escort and proceeds to the marriage altar.

If a father is not available, the bride may be escorted by a brother, uncle, stepfather, or someone special to her who can assume the role. Mothers, as will be discussed, are assuming roles analogous to fathers in the wedding ceremony.

If the children participating in a ceremony as ring bearer and flower girl are young and it is felt that they will not tolerate the service, they may be seated with family after they have executed their responsibilities. If they are old enough, they can join the wedding party and stand, as previously noted, between the officiant and the attendants. Their presence adds to the charm of the service.

A Multiplicity of Families

Processionals may have to be varied in situations where there is a multiplicity of families due to marriages and remarriages. The bride's or groom's parents may have been divorced—or widowed—and remarried. In such cases, if there is peace and good will among all concerned, the procession should involve each of the members of the extended family. A remarried mother or father of a bride or groom should proceed with her husband or his wife, respectively.

Halfway Up the Aisle

A practice has been introduced in which the bride is escorted part of the way up the aisle to a prearranged place. The groom comes forward, takes the bride, and together they approach the marriage altar. This practice is contrary to the concept of the wedding service in which both bride and groom are "brought" to the marriage experience. In another innovation, the best man leaves his place to meet and escort the maid of honor to her place. However, this practice detracts from the usual focus upon the bride and groom.

Children in the Wedding Party

In the case of a second marriage, the children, if any, may participate in the ceremony. In such cases they proceed as part of the wedding party, if serving as attendants to mother or father. If they serve as witnesses, they stand with the officiant, prior to the arrival of the wedding party.

One Variation on the Formal Wedding

Changing attitudes toward the roles of men and women in marriage has had an effect upon the traditional practice of a father escorting his daughter to the marriage altar. One variation on the formal service calls for both father and mother to escort their daughter. Though seemingly an innovation, in the Roman ritual this practice is traditional. In the European Jewish community, the men attend and escort the groom; the women escort the bride.

A Second Variation

A second variation on the formal wedding focuses upon the groom and his attendants. As previously noted, they appear with or following the officiant and take their appointed positions. Why is the bride escorted and not the groom? This practice serves as a representation of the male as the dominant figure in the marriage experience with the entire procession designed to "bring the bride to him." In other cultures, the groom is also escorted to the marriage altar. The groom may be escorted by his parents to suggest symbolically that he, too, is given in marriage. If opting for this form, provision should be made for the best man. The best man may precede the groom as the bridesmaid precedes the bride.

A Third Variation

A third variation on the formal wedding focuses upon the role parents assume at the wedding service. The formal wedding description indicates parents are seated with their guests. The wedding party arranges itself before the officiant, consisting of bride, groom, and attendants. There are parents who wish to be close to their child and the excitement of the marriage service. "As I sit and observe my child being married," muses a parent, "I wonder why I am not standing with my child, shrouded in the mystery of the ceremony, the altar, and the words of marriage."

A formal wedding may be varied to place parents among the wedding party. Parents proceed as previously indicated; however, instead of taking their seats with their guests, they continue to the marriage altar. The groom's parents take their places at the side of the groom; the bride's parents, at the side of the bride. If this variation is selected, both sets of parents should participate so as not to create the appearance of an imbalance in the ceremony, or a closer relationship to one set of parents.

A Fourth Variation

There are circumstances when escorting the bride and/or groom poses a problem. Resentment and animosity may occur among families severed by divorce or restructured by remarriage. In such cases, the bride may proceed alone. The groom may precede his bride to the altar alone. Another variation on this theme is for both the groom and the bride to be escorted by their attendants.

A Mother Serving as Escort

Traditionally, when a father is not available, the bride is escorted by a surrogate male. This practice, like so many others, derives from the male role represented symbolically during the wedding service. But certainly, if desired, a mother may escort her daughter.

The Informal Service

The informal service may take place in a sanctuary, home, or any designated place, usually with a limited number of guests. If it takes place in a sanctuary, the officiant may simply ask the attendants, calling them by name, to approach the altar and attend bride and groom. "Will you, _____, come forward to attend the groom?" And, "Will you, _____, come forward to attend the bride?" Thereafter, the groom and bride are asked to come forward. They do so together and stand before the officiant. An elaboration upon this informality may include a procession of the same participants. When the guests are few in number, they might be asked to form a circle around bride and groom.

A Second Wedding

With the increasing divorce rate, it follows that there is an increasing number of second marriages. The second marriage may be for both bride and groom, or for one of the couple planning a wedding. There is a tendency to "play down" a second wedding, a carryover from a previous time when the dissolution of a marriage reflected adversely upon husband and wife.

A second wedding should not be looked upon as a "second," but as a "new" experience. Planning for it should command and respond to the wishes and the feelings of those concerned. The decision for the

18

marriage is what is important. It is a new commitment, which should offer bride and groom fulfillments they have not previously experienced. It should be properly dramatized and celebrated.

A question often asked is, "Does the bride wear white?" Answering a question with a question, "Why not?" The white gown, symbolically, sets the bride apart. For the moment she is different from all other women in that she has chosen to make a body and soul commitment to one she loves. She is the queen, the anointed one, around whom and with whom empathetic friends celebrate. If a bride wishes to wear white—white it should be!

Children at a Wedding

Children of the bride or groom should be included in the wedding plans as guests, witnesses, or participants in the service. There are good reasons for doing so. The most important one is the help this can be for a child in his or her adjustment to a parent's remarriage. To the extent the child is brought into the wedding experience and made to feel an integral part of it—especially in the decision for marriage —the less difficult will it be for the child to feel that he or she is a full and welcome member of the new family.

One wedding took place on the patio of the new home where the two families would now live. The groom stood to the left of the bride with his son and daughter attending him. The bride stood with her two sons attending her. "Do you take this man?" she was asked. She paused, turned about, spoke first to her children, then to the children of her groom, and then to the assembled, inviting them to become part of their newness and to support one another as they begin the weaving of their lives in a togetherness. Having thus spoken, she turned back to the officiant and said, "I do!"

After another service, in which a man was married to a woman whose younger daughter stood with them, the groom took a ring from his pocket and placed it on the child's finger, thus symbolizing her inclusion in the marriage.

Double Wedding

Two sisters, two brothers, or two friends may choose to have their marriages solemnized in a single ceremony. Though some traditions object to such a practice—for it is written, "a ceremony for two brothers or two sisters on the same day should be discouraged; one celebration must not be made to interfere with another"—some brothers, sisters, and friends may want to celebrate with each other.

19

For them a double ceremony is an enrichment rather than a lessening of the celebration.

The service for the double ceremony may take one of two forms. The couples, standing together, may have the officiant read the entire service for one couple and then for the other, or the general parts of the service might be read for both couples and the personal elements, such as the vows and the ring services, alternated. First one couple is addressed and then the other.

THE WEDDING REHEARSAL

Bride and groom need not participate in a wedding rehearsal. The wedding service for them is at its best when it is spontaneous. They are not needed for the rehearsal. The responsibility of their attendants is to get them to the right place at the right time. Bride and groom should not be given words to be spoken or repeated in advance of the service. The words, like the service itself, should express the feeling that something new and exciting is happening.

A first problem in planning for a rehearsal is finding a time when members of the wedding party can be gathered together. This problem has been traditionally resolved with the prenuptial or rehearsal dinner. On an evening prior to the wedding day, the participants in the wedding ceremony are asked to join bride and groom and their families for a dinner. Before the dinner, the guests gather at the appointed place for the rehearsal. Thus, the rehearsal becomes a part of the festivities that celebrate the marriage.

A rehearsal can take place prior to the ceremony. That is the practice of hotels and catering establishments. This requires the gathering of the participants at a time before the guests arrive, allowing for a private rehearsal. The rehearsal may take the form of verbal instructions; but if the members of the wedding party are nervous, they may find verbal instructions confusing. If the wedding is formal and there are many participants, a rehearsal will certainly allay the anxieties of the participants and will work toward a rhythm that will enhance the drama of the hour.

THE WEDDING PROGRAM

An appreciated addition to a formal wedding is a wedding program, in which are included the names of the members of the wedding, the clergyperson, and a schedule of the wedding events. A program is especially useful if there are to be responsive readings and songs. It is also appreciated if the families being joined are not from the same area and do not share acquaintances.

THE WEDDING SERVICE

The request or instruction often given to the officiant for the wedding service is: "Make it simple." Everyone seems to want a "simple" service but when asked to define "simple," hardly anyone can. There is a story told of a family who planned for a formal sanctuary wedding and suggested to their clergyman that he make the service "simple." Frequently during the weeks leading to the wedding, they reminded him of their wish. When the day came, the wedding party, handsomely dressed, moved through the old, spacious sanctuary. The organ ushered in the bride and carried her to the altar, where she was joined by her groom. The celebrants were silent. The moment was packed with the anxieties of the assembled. The clergyman spoke. "Do you," he inquired of the groom, "take Susan to be your wife?" He whispered, "Yes, I do." He then turned to the bride and inquired as to her intentions. "Yes," she responded to his question. Thereupon, with a literary flourish, he pronounced them husband and wife and invoked his blessings upon them. The service was over. It was simple. It also enraged the families of bride and groom and left the guests wondering where the majesty of the service had gone.

A wedding service is, by its form and content, simple, though it is also more than that. It is responsive to the expectations of the moment. The words have been distilled through the centuries and have come to capture the mystery of the impending relationship. Though services differ one from another, the differences are slight, representing a turn of attitude or a philosophy of marriage. In all, however, they are significant and simple expressions.

Where Does the Bride Stand?

The bride, some say, stands to the right of the groom. However, it is not significant whether she stands to the right or to the left. In fact, even the posing of the question in the form of "Where does the bride stand?" rather than "How do bride and groom arrange themselves for the ceremony?" is an anathema to contemporary thinking. The position of bride and groom are important in the drama and movement of the processional. If the bride is escorted by her father and is on his

21

right hand, the groom then should approach the bride from the position of the father. In this way he will take the hand of the bride from her father without crossing in front of her. The bride will then be on his right as they approach the marriage altar. If the bride is escorted by her parents, then it will make no difference as to the direction from which the groom approaches; he will have to cross in front of one parent or the other. With the establishment of the positions of bride and groom come those of the attendants, the bride's to her side, and the groom's to his side.

There is a custom, the source and purpose of which are unknown, of seating the bride's family and their guests to the left of the sanctuary aisle and the groom's to the right. However, there is no good reason for this practice. To the contrary, a marriage is a mixing of families. Let the mixing begin with the guests as they gather to celebrate the marriage.

A Wedding Canopy

Many traditions place the bride and groom under a canopy. In Jewish tradition, the canopy takes the form of a cloth covering draped over four poles or a bower of flowers over a trellis. In effect it frames the bridal pair for the wedding service, dramatically setting the couple apart from all others. The Greeks have a bridal bower (*thalamos*), and the country people of Spain likewise frame bride and groom beneath a canopy. At a Brahmin wedding, bride and groom stand under a canopy supported by twelve pillars. In the villages of Scotland, newlyweds are escorted from the church to their home beneath a bower.

The Ring

The wedding service consists of various parts, which are common to the religious traditions of our land. Most common is the ring service. Originally, the service called for the groom to place a ring upon the bride's finger, at the same time reciting words that symbolized a binding of the marriage commitment. In recent times, this practice has changed to a reciprocal exchange of rings.

The Ring Finger.   The ring finger is usually the third finger, but the hand varies from tradition to tradition. In America, generally it is the third finger, left hand. This is in accord with the ancient Roman tradition which believed that a nerve ran directly from that finger to the heart. In Europe, it is common for the wedding band to be used as an

22

engagement ring, at which time it is worn on the third finger, left hand. Then, during the wedding ceremony, it is moved to the third finger, right hand, where it remains. In still other traditions, it is the fourth finger, with some on the left and others on the right hand.

Often a ring will be placed by the groom on the finger of his bride during the ceremony, and immediately afterwards she will remove the ring and place it upon another finger. The placing of a ring as part of the wedding ceremony takes on a mystical quality. With the recitation of the traditional words, the ring ceases to be an object and is invested with intent and sanctity. It should not be trifled with. If the bride plans to wear the ring on a certain finger, it can be placed upon that finger as part of the wedding ceremony.

As for the groom, since the exchange of rings is a contemporary innovation, no finger has been fixed as the ring finger. The groom is free to choose the finger on which he will wear his ring.

Additional rings may be used in a wedding service. A bride may ask to be married with the ring of a parent or grandparent. The ring service can, with a family ring, symbolize a promise to kin and faith, while the wedding band represents promise and commitment made by one to another.

The Ring—Converting an Embarrassment to a Symbol. In the exchange of rings, as the groom places a ring upon the finger of his bride, he may find that he cannot move the ring beyond her knuckle. He may be unnerved by this momentary frustration. The bride can come to his rescue and move the ring along her finger. To avoid this moment of embarrassment, one practice has been established that symbolizes the thought that marriage is an experience of giving and receiving. The groom initially places the ring on the finger of his bride and moves it only to the knuckle; then the bride "receives" the ring and moves it to its proper place. If the bride and groom are informed of this innovation, they will anticipate the moment and share in the placing of the ring, thus turning a potentially unnerving experience into a shared pleasure.

Is a Ring Necessary? The ring is not essential to the wedding service. Originally, the groom was expected to deliver to the bride an object of worth, representing his barter price for the bride. In the Jewish ceremony, there lingers the practice of taking the ring, placing it before the witnesses to the marriage, and having them check the worth of the object. The ring need not be a finger ring. It was in some

23

traditions too large for the wearing on a finger, and was used to hold together the bridal bouquet. John Wesley forbade the use of the ring in eighteenth-century England. In the Spanish culture, it is customary for the groom to give the "arras" (thirteen coins) to his bride in addition to the ring.

The Vows

A second part of the wedding service common to most traditions is the vows. They are public pronoucements in which bride and groom say to those assembled, "These are the promises we made to each other and now we make them known to you." Family and friends want to hear these reassuring words. The words differ from one tradition to another and also within a tradition.

In some services, prior to the vows, there is a service of intent. In this service, bride and groom are questioned as to their intentions. When they have responded affirmatively, the vows are then expressed. One of the major objections to the vows of some traditions is the use of the word "obey" as it pertains to the bride. There are also those who take exception to the phrase "as long as we shall live." In the first instance, they request the elimination of the word "obey"; in the second, they ask for a change in the wording so that it reads "as long as we shall love."

Generally, the traditional vows—the promise to love, honor, cherish, and respect one another—are always appropriate. However, if bride and groom wish, they may prepare their own vows, expressing deeply and personally the nature of their commitment.

The vows may be recited by the officiant and repeated by bride and groom, phrase by phrase, or bride and groom may recite them without the help of the officiant. There is good reason for both practices. If the officiant reads the vows, they will be heard by the assembled. Also, if the officiant is thought of as speaking for the assembled, the witnesses are then represented in the service.

The Wine Service

The wine service is an attractive element in the solemnization of a marriage. It communicates a mystical quality, a reaching toward and a sharing with the Creator in the recurring advent of Creation. In the literature it is written, "With every marriage, the Lord creates a new world—a world in which bride and groom, through their promises to each other and together to the universe, become creators with God." Bride and groom share a cup of wine. In the Hebrew service, the text reads: "As together you now drink from this cup, so may you under God's guidance, in perfect union and devotion to each other, draw contentment, comfort, and felicity from the cup of life, and thereby, may you find life's joys doubly gladdening, its bitterness sweetened, and all things hallowed by companionship and love."

In the Eastern Orthodox service, a note appears under the heading, "Symbolism of the Common Cup of Wine," which reads: "Wine is symbolic of the Marriage in Cana in Galilee, in which water is turned into wine by our Lord. The common cup itself signifies that the bride and groom shall live in accord and mutual understanding with one another, sharing equally the cup of joy and sorrow."

In Greece, the bride and groom partake of bread soaked in wine during the ceremony and handed to them by the priest.

Unitarian wedding services have, in recent times, included a wine service.

When a wedding is followed by a Communion service, the traditional "wine and bread" are offered not only to bride and groom, but to the faithful sharing in the wedding experience.

The Homily or Wedding Sermon

The wedding service does not require it, but there is a custom of extending the service with a homily or sermon. In the sermon, the officiant may weave together personal recollections or observations with instructional advice for a meaningful relationship. The homily is a literary commentary or elaboration upon the marriage theme. The officiant, at times, may lose his way in a maze of words, taxing the patience of the celebrants and encouraging the desire for simplicity or brevity. However, when expeditiously planned, both sermon and homily can and do personalize the service.

Additional Elements in the Service

In addition to the vows, rings, homily, and the sharing of a cup of wine, the service will include words of welcome, prayer for bride and groom, scriptural readings, poetic or literary selections, a pronoucement, and a benediction. For an elaboration upon each of these insertions, see the variety of services included in this volume.

THE WEDDING MUSIC

Music, a primary art form through which feelings are expressed, is generally categorized by style—classical, contemporary, sacred, rock, baroque, folk, or people music. All forms are appropriate for a wedding ceremony.

Traditions have had a hand in designating the desired, if not the proper, music for celebrating life-cycle events. Thus, many cultures within American society have musical compositions that traditionally accompany bride and groom through their wedding ceremony and celebration.

In the American tradition, Mendelssohn's *Wedding March* ("Here Comes the Bride") is generally heard ushering in the bride, and often, if the wedding party moves together, the entire wedding party. In this tradition, the Wagner march from *Tannhauser* ushers the wedding party through the recessional.

When bride and groom are knowledgeable in the language of music, they may select music that fits their mood and inclination or have music composed for their wedding ceremony.

The musical instruments for a wedding are varied and many. Because of the sanctuary, we have come to think of the organ as the primary instrument for a wedding. However, strings and winds may effectively be used to add to the drama of the wedding ceremony.

Vocal music is often programmed for the wedding service, particularly when a relative or a friend of the wedding party is musically accomplished. When vocal music is included, it fits well prior to the reading of the service. A special vocal number can be programmed for the bride's entrance. When vocal numbers are selected, the lyrics should be carefully reviewed to make certain that they "lift up" the spirit of the wedding, rather than detract from it. Although the music may be contemporary or popular, it should have a sacred quality.

It is inadvisable to introduce vocal renditions within the wedding service. They disturb the rhythm of the service and create a "dead spot" after which the excitement of the service itself must be recreated.

In the Jewish tradition, it is customary to have a cantor chant the benedictions that ordinarily would be read by the officiant. Religious traditions issue lists of appropriate music for a wedding. Some of these lists appear in this volume in the chapters on religious practices and disciplines.

THE RECESSIONAL

Today's service usually ends first with the words, "I now pronounce you husband and wife," a benediction, the embrace of bride and groom (the kiss), and the recessional.

The order of the recessional is as follows: bride and groom (bride should be reminded to retrieve her flowers which she has either given to the bridesmaid or laid upon the altar during the service), primary attendants (maid or matron of honor and best man), ring bearer and flower girl, other attendants (if any), parents of bride and groom, ushers and bridesmaids. Note that though the parents entered the room before the ushers and bridesmaids, they take their leave after the ushers and bridesmaids. It makes no difference where the parents are during the service, either standing with the wedding party or seated with the guests.

If the marriage is to be celebrated elsewhere, the wedding party may choose to depart immediately upon the conclusion of the service. They meet their guests as they reconvene either in a formal receiving line or informally, greeting the guests as they arrive.

If the marriage, is to be celebrated in the place where the wedding service is held, then a line can be formed to receive the guests as they leave the place of the service for that of the celebration, affording them an opportunity to extend their greetings and wishes to the wedding party. If they prefer the informal approach, the members of the wedding party simply mix with the guests and greet one another as they move toward and about their celebrants.

THE RECEIVING LINE

Who stands in the receiving line? There is no definitive answer to this question. Bride and groom, certainly, along with their parents. It is they, in particular, who will be receiving the greetings, good wishes, and adulation of family and friends, who share with them in the joy of witnessing the marriage of a child. Attendants may or may not be included in the receiving line. Generally, attendants prefer not to, since they are often friends of bride and groom and are not known to the guests generally. If, however, the attendants are members of the immediate family—a brother or sister, brother-in-law or sister-in-law—they may be included in the receiving line. Grandparents, if they are up to it, add to the meaningfulness of the generations in the receiving line.

A receiving line takes more time than one realizes. Allowing even for a fraction of a minute for each guest to move through the line, a guest list of 100 to 150 represents an hour or so, which can be extended if guests linger not only to greet, but also to reminisce. It is therefore advisable to have an usher take his place opposite the receiving line and encourage the guests through the line, politely urging the "story tellers" on to the reception.

THE PHOTOGRAPHER

The photographer is, in our day, an important "member" of the wedding party. He or she is interested in creating a pictorial remembrance of the event and therefore will, if possible, record each of its moments. Consequently, the photographer moves about, cutting across the sight lines of guests, standing upon chairs or pew seats, dragging equipment, signaling to assistants, popping lights—all while a service is being read. The desire to create and sustain a mood for the sacred service conflicts with the desire for the development of a pictorial story. One way to overcome this difficulty is to have pictures taken during the rehearsal or following the service. The rehearsal does not lend itself to a full picture series in that the officiant will not always participate and will certainly not rehearse the dramatic moments of the service. Following the service, separating the wedding party from the guests and holding them for a series of pictures can be difficult.

Recognizing both the need to retain the sanctity of the service and to have a pictorial remembrance of the wedding, procedures can be established that allow for the taking of pictures without disturbing the service.

The following is recommended. The photographer records the processional. Depending upon the room, the space, and the aisle, the pictures should be taken as close to the entrance as possible, avoiding movement in front of the marriage altar. Once the wedding party is in place, no flash pictures are taken, though daylight pictures from points outside of the guests' sight lines are acceptable. Under no circumstances should the photographer move about the wedding party as they stand together for the service. A time should be established, toward the end of the service, when the photographer can move about to take pictures. To be helpful, the officiant might conclude the service by inviting the guests to stand and share in the benediction. The concluding moments lend themselves well to a series of pictures that can capture the drama of the entire service.

The Handbook for Weddings, prepared by the Unitarian Church of Westport, Connecticut, states:

> No photographs are to be taken in the sanctuary prior to or during the ceremony or the recessional. This rule applies to both amateur and professional photographers. Professional photographers may photograph the bride prior to the ceremony provided this is done outside the sanctuary. Ushers will have printed cards

regarding the rule, to be given to those bringing cameras to the service. Photographs may be posed following the service.

INNOVATIVE SERVICES AND SYMBOLS

In the compelling search for the special and the different, new services have been written or tailored, a number of them available in published collections. They are, for the most part, dissertations on love, rather than literary and dramatic expressions of commitment and expectation. Analytic in their approach, they usually tell the reader what love is not. Love has many dimensions, and there is a time and a place for the discussion of those dimensions. However, the wedding service is neither the time nor the place. This should not discourage those who would have an innovative and creative service. Rather, it is to say that the question of purpose should be raised. What is it that you want to say? What should be said by the service? How might you say it, or have it said, so as to make it more meaningful than those services which have been distilled through centuries of cultural experience? An innovator must take care not to become a *latutnik*—a literary patch maker, collecting bits and pieces from a variety of sources and working them into a limping statement, lacking the rhythm, the grace, and the charm with which they were separately endowed.

Here are two innovative ceremonies. In the first, the bride and groom took a center position while the guests, including the clergyman, were seated around them. The bride spoke her love for her groom and her commitment to the life they were about to begin together. The groom responded with his affirmation of love and commitment. Then, together, they invited various guests to come forward to express their sentiments in prose or poetry. The parents were asked to invoke their blessings upon their children. Then the clergyman spoke the wedding benedictions. "We are now married," the bride and groom announced together. "Come and rejoice with us."

The second wedding took place around a table. Bride, groom, and attendants were seated. The clergyman spoke with them concerning their marriage, and asked bride and groom to affirm their love and concern for one another publicly. He then invoked upon them the traditional blessings and with that pronounced them husband and wife. Waiters, who had been standing by, then served drinks and the foods with which the wedding was celebrated.

The Lighting of Candles

A candle-lighting ceremony is now often a part of the wedding service. Two candles are placed on the marriage altar and lighted before or during the service. A third candle is added. At some point in the service, bride and groom each take one of the lighted candles and together light the third candle. They then extinguish the two candles, leaving the one burning.

The Father's (Parents') Prayer

When a father or parents escort their child to the marriage altar, at the moment of leave-taking, instead of bestowing a kiss, as is the custom, they may offer a prayer or recite words of thanksgiving.

Distributing Flowers

During the service, or immediately before the recessional, the bride ofttimes draws flowers from her bouquet and presents them to her mother and to her mother-in-law. This is a way of expressing a desire for a relationship that will embrace the entire new family.

The Handkerchief

A handkerchief can be an important item in the wedding service. The couple's attendants should carry handkerchiefs. They may not be used, but when needed, are seriously needed. The bride may burst into tears or the groom perspire vigorously. A handkerchief discreetly placed in their hands will relieve them of their discomfort.

THE FORMAL DINNER

The formal dinner is usually preceded by a reception, an hour or so affording bride, groom, and their families an opportunity to meet and greet their guests. It can be an elegant hour, comparable to the hour spent with guests at home before dinner. Drinks are served and appetites sharpened. It can also be a challenge to a caterer to prove how many dishes can possibly be squeezed into the hour. The abundance of food can mock the celebration.

Somewhere in the psyche of many people is a food anxiety. Sociologists and anthropologists have speculated on our need to tantalize the eye and tease the stomach with the appearance of food. The abundance, they suggest, is compensation for a previous time of scarcity, when the eye pleaded and the stomach prayed, a time remembered, embedded in consciousness. But was there such a time in the lives of the celebrants? Hardly! The abundance of food at many contemporary weddings has gotten out of hand. One caterer tries to outdo another. Obviously, the guests cannot possibly consume the quantities of food served during the reception hour alone, much less the dinner that follows. The eating is not a celebrating experience. It is something to be worked at—if not for the sake of the caterer, then for the host who has gone to the expense of providing an overabundance. There is a qualitative and an appreciable difference between a reception and a dinner for which the menu is carefully planned, and a reception and a dinner with a variety and an abundance that tease the guest.

The Dinner Is Announced

The dinner is announced. The guests find their seats. For three to four hours they dine, often interrupted by the blasting of music that inhibits all table conversation. The theory of contemporary music is to be contemplated. In another time, music was the environment in which one enjoyed dancing, conversing, or just being. It was the shading, the coloring of atmosphere. Today, the electronically amplified sounds command and master the individual: "You will not converse at the table! You will not relax against the background of sound! We will blow you apart!" That is precisely what happens. Not only are the guests blown apart, but blown from interactions that make time spent at the table a convivial experience.

For those who willingly respond to the music and its command, moving with it, the wedding dinner is a joyous and satisfying experience. Those who are not with it, who must sit, untalkative, waiting for each course, separated by the expanse of music, find the experience a bore. When the last course finally arrives, there is often an observable expression of relief. Why is all this necessary?

This practice is not followed throughout the land. In cities of the West and South, the dinner is served as a dinner should be: not rushed, but one course following another. Music is heard, but it is the environmental kind. When the dessert is before the guests, the time for dancing begins, at the end of which a second dessert is served. In this way, those who prefer dining and visiting with guests at the table may do so, and then leave when they wish. Those who would dance in response to the music may do so without imposing upon others.

The Reception Before the Wedding Service

Another custom comes to us from an earlier era—the reception prior to the wedding service. When transportation was less sure and

31

arrival times more flexible, guests could be expected to trickle in to a wedding household for some hours before the ceremony, which, in turn, would be delayed until most of the invited guests had arrived. Because many of the guests would have been traveling for a considerable time, refreshments were served upon their arrival.

This practice is preserved by some caterers today. However, a reception prior to a wedding service can dull the newness and dampen the excitement of the service. There is a marked difference in spirit and attitude between a congregation of guests, lean and expectant, and a gathering heady and well-fed. There can also be embarrassing moments when too much liquor at the bar blurs witness to the service.

Food Convictions and/or Restrictions

A matter properly considered is the propriety of the bride and groom imposing their tastes in food upon their guests. This occurs particularly when the bride and groom are vegetarians. In one situation, a set of parents were at odds with their vegetarian children, who insisted upon restricting the wedding celebration menu to "their" foods. The parents wanted to respect their children's wishes, but not upset the guests. The compromise solution was to offer the parents one dish of their choosing.

The same kind of situation can revolve around the question of kosher food at a Jewish wedding. For those interested, a full statement on the subject appears in the chapter on Jewish weddings.

In general, foods served at a wedding celebration should take into consideration the eating habits, likes, and dislikes of the guests. Care should be taken to make the guests comfortable. In one case the first course at a wedding celebration was artichoke vinaigrette. Many guests sat staring at the apparition, slyly looking from side to side across the adjoining tables to see what to do with it. No one ventured, until someone with a grain of courage, realizing the other guests were also totally lost, waxed humorous as he tried to quarter the vegetable —but to no avail. Finally he called for guidance. The news came back. The leaves were to be disassembled, the fleshy part dipped in a sauce, and eaten.

The Wedding Toast

Sometime during the celebration, the best man will want or be urged to offer a toast. He will try to be witty and impressive. More often than not, he will fail. If he would bear in mind the meaning and purpose of the toast, he would be more effective in its presentation.

The toast was not always the function of the best man, nor did it take its present form. During the wedding celebration, individuals would arise, call for attention, and express thoughts or feelings concerning bride, groom, or their respective families, concluding with the lifting of the cup in thanksgiving for the blessing of marriage. The best man has come to represent the guests. His toast should capture and express their feelings.

HOW MUCH SHOULD A WEDDING COST?

There is no dollar-amount answer to this question. The amount spent is better related to wealth; what might be an impossible expense for one could well suit another. One should not impoverish himself for a wedding, no matter what the temptation to overspend, to "give the bride a right and proper send-off," or to impress others. In any case, when the food is eaten, the music silent, and the guests gone, nagging regrets too often take over.

Even if the family can afford it, spending endless amounts of money does not lend sanctity or guarantee an attractive ambience for a wedding. Excess and overabundance can sour the very spirit a wedding celebration strives to evoke. One celebration ran the gamut from a voluptuous preceremony reception through a full dinner, including a staggering load of Viennese pastries, to breakfast in the morning, complete with a newspaper for each guest. This glutton's delight was in questionable taste, and one sad result was that no one talked about the wedding service, only about its gluttony.

Unfortunately, parents frequently feel threatened by their children and by their peers. In response, they may feel the need to prove themselves. More often than not, they fail—because the threat is within themselves. At the wedding of one young woman whose parents had selected one of the world's leading hotels for the marriage, everything had to be "the best of everything," in quantities to stagger the imagination. The floral arrangements alone exceeded the cost of the bride's college education. As the day of the wedding approached, the bride and her groom, increasingly apprehensive about the extravagant plans for their wedding, approached her parents and suggested to them that, while they appreciated the generosity and kindness behind the whole effort, they would be as pleased with something far simpler—and less expensive. At first, the mother and father were taken aback by the suggestion, perhaps afraid that, in some sort of polite way, their generosity was being thrown back in their faces. But

33

as they grasped the sincerity of the young people's request, they experienced a moment of revelation. They drew their children toward them, embraced them, and at once began to plan a far more modest, but in the end, much more beautiful, solemnization of the marriage.

Tithing a Wedding

When large sums are spent on a wedding celebration, the hosts may consider tithing the wedding. Tithing is a biblical tradition which calls for giving up a tithe—ten percent—of one's good fortune to the community or to the needy. A number of religious traditions call for tithing. Making a contribution equal to ten percent of the wedding's cost can evoke a feeling of sharing that gives the whole celebration a quality of the sacred, and a sense that others, far beyond the list of guests, will have reason to be glad that the wedding took place. The tithe may be directed to any worthy cause, as decided by those involved in paying the expenses, and delivered with a note stating that the gift is sent as an expression both of thanksgiving and of a desire to share their blessing with others.

Who Pays for the Wedding?

It has been the custom for the family of the bride to assume the costs of the wedding. Today, exclusions have developed allowing for or calling upon the groom or his family to pay for such items as the prenuptial dinner, the fee for the service, the bride's flowers, and sometimes the liquor. The expectation that the bride's family will plan and pay for the wedding has its roots in a social system that has changed radically. It was the need and the anxiety to marry off one's daughters, offering up the best terms in this interest, that made it a bride's wedding. It is time to review this practice in the light of present-day attitudes and to suggest that the planning and the payment for the wedding should not be solely the bride's family's prerogative.

The cost of a wedding depends upon the guest list. The more guests, the greater the cost. Since it has been the bride's family that has traditionally planned and paid for the wedding, the guests, for the most part, included the bride's family and their friends. The groom's family is given a number of places on the list, usually a fraction of the total. In order to obtain a larger representation, families have offered to "pay their share" or share the cost. This kind of an incursion on an ancient tradition often results in embarrassment. Obviously, the ancient practice is archaic. There is no longer any reason for it. To the contrary, the spirit of these times suggests the wedding costs and planning be shared by the families involved.

34

To emphasize the propriety of this approach, it is noted that many brides work to keep their husbands in school until their training is completed. Other brides and grooms work in order to provide home and goods for their living together. These sharing experiences should begin with the planning for the wedding and the paying of all the associated costs. It is also conceivable that one family is more affluent than the other. Sharing, therefore, should take into consideration the wherewithal of both families.

Insuring the Wedding Celebration

Insurance coverage for a loss resulting from cancellation, postponement, curtailment, or removal of a planned celebration to an alternate premise is now available. The benefits, as outlined by one insurance agency, are as follows:

Catered Affair Cancellation Insurance covers you with respect to (1) the possible loss of your deposit and (2) the possible loss of profits to the caterer for which you may become liable due to any cause beyond your control or the control of specified principal participants in your affair.

> You are covered for up to, but not exceeding, the total contract price of your catered affair.
>
> You are covered if there is a serious illness, disability or death involving specified principal participants...if severe weather necessitates cancellation or causes curtailment...even if the prospective bride and groom decide "to call the whole thing off."

The premium for party insurance is quoted at $10 per $1,000 with a minimum premium of $60. Since there are exclusions in this kind of insurance, those considering insuring their plans should examine the policy carefully, taking note of the qualifications and exclusions listed in the small print.

Fees and Payments for Services

Payment for services generally will be agreed upon and contracted for. It is advised that contracts should not be entered into until the essential details for the wedding ceremony and celebration have been established. Deposits are required in many contractual arrangements. If at all possible, those entering into these contracts should have a clause inserted that allows for the cancellation of the contract under special conditions and for a change of date if circumstances require.

Payment for a wedding service is often fraught with embarrassment for both groom and clergy. There is a prevailing notion that religious services are a natural or communal right. Aligned with that notion is the feeling that religious services need not be paid for. Accordingly, there is the custom of giving the officiant a gratuity—a free-will offering.

In general practice, however, many religions make a distinction between families associated with them and those not associated. In the case of associates (parishioners, members), fees are not charged for religious services. When non-members ask a clergyperson and religious community for their services, charges are made, depending upon the nature of the services rendered. It is best for all concerned that these charges be made known at the time the wedding is confirmed and scheduled. Payment should be made prior to the wedding day. The aftermath of a wedding service is not the time for wedding celebrants to deal with financial aspects of the wedding.

If fees and charges are deemed by those requesting a service to be beyond their means, they should so indicate. The charge will be revised. There is a general conviction that a cost or charge should not be an impediment to a religious service. Let it be understood, however, that the form and manner of the celebration will suggest whether or not fees and charges are appropriate.

Robert N. Rodenmayer, writing in his volume, *I, John, Take You, Mary,* says:

> There should be no such thing as a fee for a clergyman officiating at a wedding. ... It is a family act, for and by the family. However, it is appropriate for a couple to make a thank-offering for what they have received. Also if one has required special services from organist, sexton, etc., it is not unreasonable to find that they have standard fees. No church should have a charge for the use of the building by its own people, although churches which attract weddings from outside their own membership may, and often do, require prescribed payments for use and services.

THE HONEYMOON

Some couples decide not to plan a honeymoon; instead, they want to "wing it"—just take off and let love and fancy be their guide. This sounds romantic and might under certain circumstances prove to be venturesome, exciting, and satisfying. In most cases, however, lack of planning for a honeymoon results in unpleasantness that can only mar the wedding day. Weddings take place on weekends and holidays, times when people are on the move, especially in the popular vacation months of the year. Hotels and resorts are often booked. Looking for a place, and a particular one at that, may become tedious and disappointing. To avoid disappointment and discomfort, bride and groom should make certain that their honeymoon plans are in order. If the plans have been made some time in advance of their wedding day, they should reconfirm all reservations a day or so prior to the wedding.

ON RETAINING OR HYPHENATING FAMILY NAMES

From time immemorial, common practice has been for a bride to give up her family name for that of her husband. Recently, though, many brides have sought ways to retain their family names. Their motivations are varied. In some cases, the bride may have established herself in a profession or enterprise that bears or is identified by her name. In other cases, brides feel pride in their families. Finally, many women feel that they should not have to give up a name because of a long tradition of a bride's subservience in a marriage relationship.

A bride may legally retain her family name after marriage, or bride and groom may hyphenate their names, retaining both as a single name. Retaining two different names may pose problems in the commercial world—utility companies, banks and credit institutions, tax bureaus, rental agencies, etc. Many institutions, however, are slowly coming around to understand and respond to what is now considered a reasonable request on the part of women. As for hyphenating, a question arises concerning the order of the names. The recommended approach is to test the names euphonically. Speak them in one order and then the other. The form most pleasing to the ear can prevail.

The right of a bride to retain her name, or for a couple to hyphenate their names, is, in the state of New York, found in the Civil Rights Law, Section 60, which reads: "Under the common law, a person may change his or her name at will as long as there is no fraud, misrepresentation, or interference with the rights of others."

37

DEATH IN THE FAMILY

If a parent, grandparent, or sibling dies prior to a wedding, what is the propriety with regard to the wedding plans? The answer to the question will vary with religious groups and from family to family. If the death is expected, that person may have felt comfortable discussing the eventuality, so that a plan could be made with his or her wishes taken into account. If the death is sudden, then the family needs to talk about the situation as soon as it is sensibly possible for them to do so. Many things need be taken into account, among them the time between the death and the wedding date, the expectations of the guests, and the nature of the wedding plans. Of these, the expectations of the guests is perhaps the most important. If holding the wedding as scheduled will be deemed appropriate by the guests, then it probably is appropriate. If even a minority of the guests would be disturbed, then probably, within their tradition, the marriage ought to be postponed.

Since a wedding is, depending upon the tradition, a sacrament, a public worship service, or an act of sanctification, a service can properly take place. However, the usual fanfare that attends a wedding should be eliminated, and the religious aspect of the wedding emphasized, as a mark of respect for the deceased. The meal following the service should be limited to the quiet gathering of the witnesses to the marriage sharing in a meal of "thanksgiving" opened and closed with prayer.

PREPARATION FOR MARRIAGE

Until recently, the thought that marriage was something to prepare for, study, and learn about in advance of a wedding was widely rejected. After all, when one is ready for marriage or thinks one is ready, then that is that! The thinking behind this approach derives from the assumption that marriage comes naturally and is something for which people are innately equipped.

In fact, marriage is the most difficult and demanding of all human relations, charged with fulfillment and frustration, delight and disappointment, far beyond any inborn understanding or expectation. The chilling fact that every second or third marriage ends in divorce is the most compelling testimony to this truth.

Above all, problems in marriage arise from expectations that are unfulfilled, fantasies unrealized, preconceptions unmet. Contemporary society—in its literature, theatre, advertising, and folklore—inspires images and beliefs about "how it's going to be" that turn out to be mirages. If there is a mutual understanding of what marriage involves and if expectations are reasonable, the erosion of marriage relationships can be prevented.

Examples of Unfulfilled Expectations

In defense of himself, he said, "But I give her all the money she needs. Why does she complain so?" She responds, "Why must I ask him whenever I need funds and stand by as he doles out my allowance?" Upon further inquiry we learn that, as a child, she found the money relationship in her family deeply disturbing. In her marriage, she thought, she would be freed from that agony. Marriage and husband, however, represented a continuation of a disturbing experience.

Neatness is one of the hobgoblins of marriage. She was deeply disturbed by his habits, exclaiming in exasperation, "He never puts the toilet seat down." This was but the tip of the iceberg. There was the toothpaste tube, squeezed from the middle, laundry on the floor—all the housekeeping details of marriage, quite unromantic and unexpected. He confessed that, in his mother's home, these were but triffles, hardly causing a wave of disturbance. He did not know, did not understand. She said he was insensitive.

"Must I take your friends because I married you? I can't stand them, especially your sister. She's a creep. I wish you would spend less time with her." Or: "I don't mind that old crowd of yours, but must you bring them into the house?" "Criticize my friends and you criticize me. They are my judgments and you're attacking them. Reject them and I am rejected!"

How does one avoid these tensions which eventually lead to harsh words, bruised feelings, and an erosion of a relationship?

There is no question but that a marriage would be well served if bride and groom took advantage of programs that offer training in preparation for marriage. Each would come to understand his/her own expectations and the expectations of the other. Because the roles of husband and wife are radically changing in contemporary society, the problems of expectations are further intensified as old patterns are explored, criticized, and condemned.

The syllabus of one premarriage program offers the following topics for discussion and consideration:

39

- Why Marriage? The motivations
- What Is Love? The dynamics
- Physiology—Aspects of sexuality
- Psychology of the Sexes
- Communications
- Moral Issues—Premarital sex, birth control, abortion, divorce

ON THE PURPOSE OF MARRIAGE

Much has been and will be said concerning the nature and purpose of marriage.

A biblical episode, more than most writings, is incisive in its commentary upon the marriage purpose. In the story of Creation, Adam, the man, was created as the last of God's ventures and placed in the Garden of Eden—a luxurious place, especially designed for him, filled with the good things of life. Adam was not responsive to the wealth of his surroundings, the gold and precious stones washed up by one of the four rivers that flowed out of the garden. He was lonely, unfulfilled. God, thereupon, to improve His handiwork, created woman. When Adam was deep in sleep, God opened his rib cage, took a rib and with it made woman. An imaginative myth? Perhaps—but the language and the intent of the story are of significance. As the Lord prepares to create woman, He says, "I will make this woman *kenegdo*." An interesting word in that it translates as either *against* or *opposite* this man! If the Lord's intention was to extract Adam from his loneliness, should He not have made this woman to comfort and attend this man? It is this special word *kenedgo* that directs us to the intent and purpose of the marriage relationship.

A human being is a promise made by the Lord to the universe. In and with every human being there is the hope that his/her life will in some measure become a creative moment in the on-going process of the universe. Regrettably, most humans fail their own promise. This is a confession that we readily make. Said the Lord, "I give this woman to this man *kenegdo*"—to oppose, to urge and to inspire the fulfillment of the promise that is within him. Conversely, this woman is given to this man in a mutual relationship in which the promise inherent in her, will, by virtue of marriage, become manifest in her life. Together, then, by this interaction the promise and fulfillment of husband and wife can become a creative force for the universe as a whole. In this sense they become co-workers with God in the process of creation.

WHAT TO DO AND WHEN...
A WEDDING CHECKLIST

Once the decision to marry is made, the prospective bride and groom—and their families—have much to think about and many details to attend to in preparation for the wedding. Careful and timely planning can help eliminate some of the natural tension and anxiety from this emotional occasion.

Six Months to One Year Before the Wedding:

- Decide what kind of wedding service and reception you want.
- Talk over your plans with the officiating clergy.
- Determine your budget for the wedding, reception, and honeymoon.
- Reserve locations for the wedding service and reception. Deposits may be required.
- Compile invitation lists with your families.
- Choose attendants.
- Start shopping for wedding dress and accessories, attendants' gowns, and tuxedo rentals.
- Select caterer, florist, and photographer.
- Decide on music for wedding and reception, and book appropriate musicians.
- Begin planning your honeymoon. If you plan to travel outside the United States, you may need passports, visas, and innoculations.
- Arrange for vacations from work for wedding and honeymoon.
- Register at a local store's bridal registry.
- Send engagement notice to local newspaper.

Three to Four Months Before the Wedding:

- Participate in premarital counseling with clergy or support group.
- Finalize the guest list and confirm details of the reception.
- Look at wording in various sample invitation books.
- Order invitations, announcements, and thank-you notes.
- Pick up envelopes for invitations in advance and address them.
- Determine amount of postage needed for invitations and buy stamps.
- Decide where you will live after the wedding and make necessary arrangements.

Two Months Before the Wedding:

- Select wedding rings and allow time for engraving.
- Mail invitations. Send information regarding local motel accommodations to out-of-town guests. Also include a map of your area.
- Keep a record of gifts received and write thank-you notes promptly.
- Make appointments for physical exams and blood tests.
- Arrange date to obtain marriage license.
- Reserve any rental equipment (i.e., videotape recorder).
- Record responses to invitations as they come in.
- Arrange fittings for bridal gown, attendants' dresses, and tuxedos.

One Month Before the Wedding:

- Order wedding cake.
- Order flowers for wedding service and reception.
- Have final fittings for wedding clothes.
- If wedding portrait is to be done prior to wedding day, have it done at this time.
- Look into insurance policies for both of you and for your new home.
- Plan bachelors' and bridesmaids' parties.
- Buy gifts for attendants.
- Complete shopping for wedding and honeymoon.
- Arrange transportation for wedding party, out-of-town guests, and local guests who may need assistance.
- Continue to record gifts and write thank-you notes.
- Buy gifts for each other.

Two Weeks Before the Wedding:

- Get new home ready. Send changes of address.
- If name changes are planned, do so on important documents, driver's license, and credit cards.
- Confirm guest list with caterer.
- Finalize seating for the reception.
- Make appointment with hairdresser.
- Arrange for wedding rehearsal.
- Try on all clothes to be sure everything is ready.
- Send wedding announcement to local newspaper(s).
- Continue to record gifts and write thank-you notes.

One Week Before the Wedding:

- Confirm all arrangements with officiating clergy.
- Go over all details with caterer, photographer, musicians, florist, and anyone else you have engaged for the occasion.
- Have parties for attendants.
- Attend rehearsal and rehearsal dinner.
- Prepare announcements for mailing on wedding day.
- Pack and do last-minute errands.
- Reconfirm honeymoon reservations.
- Enjoy yourselves!

The
Protestant
Wedding

Protestantism covers a wide range of religious convictions and practices, from biblically oriented confessions to liberal interpretations of religious experience. Differences in theology and practice are reflected in the wedding services of each denomination. This chapter presents texts, rituals, customs, and practices pertaining to a variety of Protestant wedding services.

The Protestant wedding differs from that of other religions in that it is a worship service through which the will of God is served and the Lordship of Jesus is proclaimed. The wedding guests are participants in the service and witnesses to the ecclesiastical solemnization of the marriage contract. They share in the service with hymns, scriptural readings, and responses to the couple's exchange of vows.

There are few restrictions regarding the time and place of a Protestant wedding, though certain times may conflict with major religious services or celebrations. A minister can advise a couple on the propriety of the date and time desired. Because the wedding is a worship service, a church setting is appropriate. However, a home, hall, or outdoor location may also be suitable. It is customary and proper for the prospective bride and groom to discuss their wedding plans with a minister before the date is announced. Certain groups require the couple to give notice of their wedding date. The Episcopal canon requires that notice be given at least 30 days before the scheduled event. In addition, some disciplines require premarital counseling prior to the actual service. Thus, for example, a United Methodist wedding should be scheduled four to six months in advance, to allow for this counseling.

Protestants who have been previously married and divorced are permitted to marry again, though some denominations may require dispensation from Church officials for the marriage. An Episcopal minister must obtain the consent of the Bishop prior to solemnizing the marriage of a divorced person.

WEDDING CUSTOMS

Since the Protestant wedding is a worship service, the witnesses, or congregation, stand when the bride enters and remain standing during the service. In lengthy or elaborate services, in which readings and a sermon or homily are included, the bride, groom, and congregation may be seated during the readings and the sermon or homily.

In those disciplines that stipulate where the bride and groom are to stand in relation to the minister, the groom is to the minister's left and the bride to the right.

In order for the congregation to enjoy full participation in the wedding worship service, the bride and groom may prepare and distribute a program listing the order of the service, including hymns, readings, responses, and prayers. The program should also include the names of all participants in the wedding service. As an additional gesture, the bride and groom may also include a personal message to welcome their guests and provide them with last-minute details of the celebration.

THE WEDDING SERVICE

The wedding service may include most or all of these parts. Detailed explanations of each follow.

1. **The Beginning**
   Words of Welcome
   Scriptural and Other Readings
   Homily or Sermon
2. **The Marriage**
   Declaration of Intent
   The Blessing of the Congregation upon the Bride and Groom
   "Who Gives This Bride Away?"
   Vows
   Presentation of Ring(s)
   Announcement
   Prayer

3. Epilogue
   Thanksgiving and Lord's Prayer
   Holy Communion
   Agape Meal
4. Conclusion
   Benediction

The **words of welcome** may be an informal greeting to the bride, groom, and witnesses to the marriage, or a formal statement. One often heard follows:

> Dearly beloved: We are gathered together in the sight of God, and in the face of this company, to join together this man and this woman in holy matrimony [*the statement is more effective if the names of the bride and groom are inserted*], which is an estate instituted of God and made honorable by the faithful keeping of good men and women in all time. It is, therefore, not by any to be entered into unadvisedly or lightly, but reverently, discreetly, soberly, and in the fear of God. Into this holy estate, these two persons come now to be joined. If any can show just cause why they may not be lawfully joined together, let him now speak or forever hold his peace.

The opening statement may be literary. The words of Kahlil Gibran are often requested for a wedding service:

> Love one another, but make not a bond of love:
> Let it rather be a moving sea between the shores of your souls.
> Fill each other's cup but drink not from one cup.
> Give one another of your bread but eat not from the same loaf.
> Sing and dance together and be joyous, but let each one of you be alone,
> Even as the strings of a lute are alone though they quiver with the same music.
> Give your hearts, but not into each other's keeping.
> For only the hand of Life can contain your hearts.
> And stand together, yet not too near together:
> For the pillars of the temple stand apart,
> And the oak tree and the cypress grow not in each other's shadow.
> But let there be spaces in your togetherness,
> And let the winds of the heavens dance between you.
> Love one another, but make not a bond of love.

Scriptural readings may be selected from both the Old and New Testaments. However, readings need not be limited to Scripture.

46

Other selections appropriate to a marriage celebration may, with the approval of the minister, be included in the service. The readings may be offered by the minister, by members of the wedding party, or by friends of the bride and groom.

The **homily** or **sermon** emphasizes the Christian aspect of the marriage, as well as the responsibilities involved. It is also a means to personalize the service. When the minister has known the bride and groom and their families for some time, he or she may want to express personal feelings for them either in a "lesson of faith" or in words of confidence in the marriage. The homily or sermon sometimes uses the dramatic forms of music and dance.

During the wedding service, the bride and groom are called upon to make a **Declaration of Intent,** to state their intentions. An Episcopalian couple signs a statement prior to the ceremony:

> We, _____ and _____, desiring to receive the blessing of Holy Matrimony in the Church, do solemnly declare that we hold marriage to be a lifelong union of husband and wife as set forth in the liturgical forms authorized by this Church.
>
> We believe it is for the purpose of mutual fellowship, encouragement, and understanding; for the procreation of children and their physical and spiritual nurture; and for the safeguarding and benefit of society.
>
> And we do engage ourselves, as far as in us lies, to make our utmost effort to establish this relationship and to seek God's help thereto.
>
> *Signatures:*   *Date:*

During the service, the form and language of the Intent vary. A traditional form is:

> *Will you have this man/woman to be your wedded husband/wife, to live together in holy matrimony? Will you love him/her, comfort him/her, honor and keep him/her in sickness and in health, in sorrow and in joy, and, forsaking all others, be faithful to him/her as long as you both shall live?*

The Intent may also be as brief as the minister's statement concerning the purpose of the service: "This celebration is the outward token of a sacred and inward union of the hearts which the Church does bless and the State makes legal ... a union created by loving purpose and kept by abiding will. ..." The minister then asks the bride and groom: "Is it in this spirit and for this purpose that you have come here to be joined together?" The bride and groom respond: "Yes, I have."

47

The **blessing of the congregation upon the bride and groom** is a response to the Intent by the worshipers. The minister asks the congregants: "Will you lend your hearts and your concerns to these two persons, upholding them in their resolve and encouraging them in their marriage?" The congregation responds: "We will," or with a fuller statement.

"Who gives this bride away?" is part of an ancient tradition, questioned today, in which the bride was "given" to her groom, usually by her father. The custom is reminiscent of a time when the legal aspect of the marriage dominated the service and the bride was considered to be the property of her husband. When John Wesley prepared his service for American Methodists, he omitted this practice. However, today there are Methodist and other Protestant services in which the question is asked, and there are brides who choose to have their fathers escort them to the marriage altar and respond to the question, "Who gives this bride to this man?"

As with the Intent, the words of the **vows** vary from one discipline to another. In recent years, more and more couples preparing for marriage have been writing their own vows. These vows usually take the form of a statement in which the couple express their love for, and elaborate upon their commitment to, each other. The vows may also be a poem which the bride and groom recite or read responsively. Couples planning for marriage may be encouraged in this endeavor so that their vows express their mutual commitment more meaningfully. During the recitation of vows, the bride and groom join their right hands. A traditional vow is:

> I take you to be my wife/husband,
> To have and to hold, from this day forward,
> For better, for worse, for richer, for poorer,
> In sickness and in health, to love and to cherish,
> Till death do us part.
> This is my solemn vow
> According to God's holy ordinance;
> And thereto I plight you my troth.

A contemporary vow reads:

> I acknowledge my love and respect for you and invite you to share
> my life as I hope to share yours. I promise always to recognize you
> as an individual and always to be conscious of your development
> as well as my own. I shall seek through kindness and understand-
> ing to achieve with you the life we have envisioned.

The **presentation of rings** comes at this point in the wedding service. It is interesting to note that many religious leaders in the past shunned ornaments and jewelry. John Wesley forbade the use of the ring in his marriage services. Generally, the bride's wedding band is placed on the third finger of her left hand, though the Presbyterian tradition calls for the ring to be placed on the fourth finger of the left hand. In a Methodist ceremony, if the groom is to receive a ring, it is also placed upon the third finger of the left hand.

When the rings are given or exchanged, the bride and groom may speak any of these words or choose words of their own:

With this ring, I thee wed, in the Name of God. AMEN.

With this ring I wed you, and pledge my faithful love.

I give you this ring as a sign of my vow, and with all that I am, and all that I have, I honor you.

This ring I give you in token and pledge of our constant faith and abiding love.

With this ring I thee wed; in the Name of the Father, and of the Son, and of the Holy Spirit. AMEN.

The service ends with an **announcement:**

For as much as you have consented together in wedlock, and have witnessed the same before God and this company, and thereto have engaged and pledged yourselves to each other, and have declared the same by giving and receiving a ring and by joining hands, I pronounce that you are man and wife.

In recent years, many couples have objected strongly to the phrase "man and wife." Most announcements have been amended to read "husband and wife."

For as much as you have pledged yourselves to each other in the presence of this company, I do now, by virtue of the authority vested in me by this State, pronounce that you are husband and wife.

Now that you have given yourselves to each other by solemn vows, with the joining of hands and the giving of rings, I announce that you are husband and wife in the Name of the Father, and of the Son, and of the Holy Spirit. Those whom God has joined together, let no one separate.

Many **prayers** are appropriate for the wedding service. Selections may depend on the denomination of the officiating minister and personal preferences. Some of the prayers are religious in concept and language while others are literary. Here are examples of these kinds of prayers:

> Almighty God, our heavenly Father, the Fountain of all joy, from Whom cometh every good and perfect gift, we thank Thee for the sacred and tender ties which these, Thy children, have now taken upon themselves. May all their loved ones, here assembled, or in absence, remembering them, ever continue to rejoice in the bonds which unite them. We ask for them that the inspiration of this hour may abide throughout their lives, and that in joy or in sorrow, in pleasant ways, or in the midst of trials, they may ever acknowledge Thy guiding hand and be obedient to Thy laws. May they be comfort and joy, counsel and strength, to each other through all the chances and changes of this world. Hand in hand and heart with heart, trusting in each other and in Thee, united not by man, but by Thy holy spirit, may they walk together along the pathway of life in faith, hope, and love; and may the benediction of heaven crown their happiness on earth. AMEN.

> •

> Now you will feel no rain, for each of you will be shelter to the other. Now you will feel no cold, for each of you will be warmth to the other. Now there is no loneliness for you. Now you are two bodies, but there is one life before you.
> Go now to your dwelling place, to enter into the days of your togetherness.
> And may your days be good and long upon the earth.
>
> *(An Apache prayer)*

> •

> Let me not to the marriage of true minds
> Admit impediments. Love is not love
> Which alters when it alteration finds,
> Or bends with the remover to remove:
> O, no! It is an ever-fix'd mark,
> That looks on tempests and is never shaken;
> It is the star to every wandering bark,
> Whose worth's unknown, although his height be taken.
> Love's not Time's fool, though rosy lips and cheeks
> Within his bending sickle's compass come;
> Love alters not with his brief hours and weeks,
> But bears it out even to the edge of doom.
> If this be error and upon me prov'd,
> I never writ, nor no man ever lov'd.
>
> *(Shakespearean sonnet 116)*

The basic wedding service is complete with the announcement "husband and wife." However, an ending consisting of a **service of thanksgiving, holy communion,** or an **Agape Meal** (Love Feast) may be added. Holy communion is always a part of the Episcopal service. The ancient tradition of the Agape Meal, or the meal following the wedding service, had long ago fallen into disuse, but has been revived in various Protestant disciplines. The meal may be considered an integral part of the ceremony, including special prayers and blessings in which the bride and groom participate. In its contemporary form, members of the wedding party distribute symbolic foods chosen for the Agape Meal to the guests. As part of the meal, the bride and groom may express their joy by sharing their blessing with the assembled. Families of the bride and groom may choose to offer a portion of the meal as a gift to the poor (see "Tithing," page 34 above). Another choice is to make the Agape Meal part of the wedding feast. Performed at the beginning of the feast, the Agape Meal gives the event a sacred quality and makes it an integral part of the wedding ceremony.

The **benediction** is the final blessing, which then serves to dismiss the congregation. Following the benediction, it is customary for the bride and groom to embrace one another and to kiss. However, there are disciplines that frown upon this practice.

Following are a number of wedding services published in their entirety. They have been selected to represent a variety of Protestant denominations.

AN EPISCOPAL MARRIAGE SERVICE

The Celebration and Blessing of a Marriage

PRIEST *to People:* Dearly Beloved: We have come together in the presence of God to witness and bless the joining together of this man and woman in holy matrimony. The bond and covenant of marriage was established by God in Creation, and our Lord Jesus Christ adorned this manner of life by His presence and first miracle at a wedding in Cana of Galilee. It signifies to us the mystery of the union between Christ and His Church, and Holy Scripture commends it to be honored among all people.

The union of husband and wife in heart, body, and mind is intended by God for their mutual joy; for the help and comfort given one another in prosperity and adversity; and, when it is

51

God's will, for the procreation of children and their nurture in the knowledge and love of the Lord.

Therefore, marriage is not to be entered into unadvisedly or lightly, but reverently, deliberately, and in accordance with the purposes for which it was instituted by God.

Into this holy union _____ and _____ now come to be joined. *(Priest uses full names here, but only first names from this point on.)* If any of you can show just cause why they may not lawfully be married, speak now; or else forever hold your peace.

PRIEST *to Bride and Groom:* I require and charge you both, here in the presence of God, that if either of you know any reason why you should not be united in marriage lawfully, and in accordance with God's Word, you do now confess it.

The Declaration of Consent

PRIEST *first to Groom and then to Bride:* _____, will you have this woman/man to be your wife/husband; to live together in the covenant of marriage? Will you love her/ him, comfort her/him, honor and keep her/him, in sickness and in health; and, forsaking all others, be faithful to her/him as long as you both shall live?

GROOM/BRIDE: I will.

PRIEST *to People:* Will all of you witnessing these promises do all in your power to uphold these two persons in their marriage?

PEOPLE: We will.

The Ministry of the Word

PRIEST: The Lord be with you.

PEOPLE: And also with you.

PRIEST: Let us pray. O gracious and everliving God, You have created us male and female in Your image: Look mercifully upon this man and this woman who come to You seeking Your blessing, and assist them with Your grace, that with true fidelity and steadfast love they may honor and keep the promises and vows they make; through Jesus Christ our Savior, Who lives and reigns with You in the unity of the Holy Spirit, one God, for ever and ever. AMEN.

One or more of the following passages from Holy Scripture is read. A passage from the Gospel concludes the Readings.

- Genesis 1:26-28 (Male and female He created them)
- Genesis 2:4-9,15-24 (A man cleaves to his wife and they become one flesh)

52

- Song of Solomon 2:10-13; 8:6-7 (Many waters cannot quench love)
- Tobit 8:5b-8 [New English Bible] (That she and I may grow old together)
- I Corinthians 13:1-13 (Love is patient and kind)
- Ephesians 3:14-19 (The Father from whom every family is named)
- Ephesians 5:1-2,21-33 (Walk in love, as Christ loved us)
- Colossians 3:12-17 (Love which binds everything together in harmony)
- I John 4:7-16 (Let us love one another for love is of God)

Between the Readings, a Psalm, hymn, or anthem may be sung or said. Appropriate Psalms are 67, 127, 128.

- Matthew 5:1-10 (The Beatitudes)
- Matthew 5:13-16 (You are the light ... Let Your light so shine)
- Matthew 7:21,24-29 (Like a wise man who built his house upon the rock)
- Mark 10:6,13-16 (They are no longer two but one)
- John 15:9-12 (Love one another as I have loved you)

The Marriage

BRIDE AND GROOM *face each other and, joining right hands, repeat (use of one of these vows is mandatory):* In the Name of God, I, _____, take you, _____, to be my husband/wife, to have and to hold from this day forward, for better for worse, for richer for poorer, in sickness and in health, to love and to cherish, until we are parted by death. This is my solemn vow.

or:

I, _____, take thee, _____, to be my wedded husband/wife, to have and to hold from this day forward, for better for worse, for richer for poorer, in sickness and in health, to love and to cherish, till death do us part, according to God's holy ordinance; and thereto I plight/give thee my troth.

They loosen their hands.

Priest may ask God's blessing on a ring or rings as follows:

PRIEST: Bless, O Lord, this ring to be a sign of the vows by which this man and this woman have bound themselves to each other; through Jesus Christ our Lord. AMEN.

Giver places the ring on the ring finger of the other's hand and says:

GROOM/BRIDE: _____, I give you this ring as a symbol of my vow, and with all that I am, and all that I have, I honor you, in the Name of the Father, and of the Son, and of the Holy Spirit [*or:* in the Name of God].

Weddings

PRIEST _joins the right hands of Groom and Bride and says:_ Now that
_____ and _____ have given themselves to each other by
solemn vows, with the joining of hands and the giving and receiving of a ring, I pronounce that they are husband and wife, in
the Name of the Father, and of the Son, and of the Holy Spirit.
Those whom God has joined together let no one put asunder.
PEOPLE: AMEN.

The Prayers

PRIEST _to standing People:_ Let us pray together in the words our Saviour
taught us.
PEOPLE and PRIEST:
Our Father in heaven,
hallowed be Your Name,
Your kingdom come,
Your will be done,
on earth as in heaven.

Give us today our daily bread.
Forgive us our sins,
as we forgive those
who sin against us.

Save us from the time of trial,
and deliver us from evil.
For the kingdom, the power,
and the glory are Yours,
now and for ever. AMEN.

If Communion is to follow, some Prayers may be omitted here.

PRIEST: Let us pray. Eternal God, Creator and Preserver of all life,
Author of salvation, and Giver of all grace: Look with favor
upon the world You have made, and for which Your Son gave
His life, and especially upon this man and this woman whom
You made one flesh in Holy Matrimony. AMEN.

Give them wisdom and devotion in the ordering of their
common life, that each may be to the other a strength in need,
a counselor in perplexity, a comfort in sorrow, and a companion in joy. AMEN.

Grant that their wills may be so knit together in Your will,
and their spirits in Your Spirit, that they may grow in love and
peace with You and one another all the days of their life.
AMEN.

Give them grace, when they hurt each other, to recognize
and acknowledge their fault, and to seek each other's forgiveness and Yours. AMEN.

54

Make their life together a sign of Christ's love to this sinful and broken world, that unity may overcome estrangement, forgiveness heal guilt, and joy conquer despair. AMEN.

(Optional:) Bestow on them, if it is Your will, the gift and heritage of children, and the grace to bring them up to know You, to love You, and to serve You. AMEN.

Give them such fulfillment of their mutual affection that they may reach out in love and concern for others. AMEN.

Grant that all married persons who have witnessed these vows may find their lives strengthened and their loyalties confirmed. AMEN.

Grant that the bonds of our common humanity, by which all Your children are united one to another, and the living to the dead, may be so transformed by Your grace, that Your will may be done on earth as it is in heaven; where, O Father, with Your Son and the Holy Spirit, You live and reign in perfect unity, now and for ever. AMEN.

The Peace

PRIEST: The peace of the Lord be always with you.

PEOPLE: And also with you.

A PRESBYTERIAN MARRIAGE SERVICE

MINISTER *to Congregation:* Dearly beloved: We are assembled here in the presence of God, to join this man and this woman in holy marriage; which is instituted of God, regulated by His commandments, blessed by our Lord Jesus Christ, and to be held in honor among all men. Let us therefore reverently remember that God has established and sanctified marriage, for the welfare and happiness of mankind. Our Savior has declared that a man shall leave his father and mother and cleave unto his wife. By His apostles, He has instructed those who enter into this relation to cherish a mutual esteem and love; to bear with each other's infirmities and weaknesses; to comfort each other in sickness, trouble, and sorrow; in honesty and industry to provide for each other, and for their household, in temporal things; to pray for and encourage each other in the things which pertain to God; and to live together as the heirs of the grace of life.

Foreasmuch as these two persons have come hither to be made one in this holy estate, if there be any here present

who knows any just cause why they may not lawfully be joined in marriage, I require him now to make it known, or ever
after to hold his peace.

MINISTER *to Bride and Groom:* I charge you both, before the great God,
the Searcher of all hearts, that if either of you know any reason why you may not lawfully be joined together in marriage, you now confess it. For be well assured that if any persons are joined together otherwise than as God's Word
allows, their union is not blessed by Him.

MINISTER *(if no impediment appears):* Let us pray. Almighty and ever-
blessed God, Whose presence is the happiness of every condition, and Whose favor hallows every relation: We beseech
Thee to be present and favorable unto these Thy servants,
that they may be truly joined in the honorable estate of marriage, in the covenant of their God.

As Thou has brought them together by Thy providence,
sanctify them by Thy Spirit, giving them a new frame of
heart fit for their new estate; and enrich them with all grace,
whereby they may enjoy the comforts, undergo the cares,
endure the trials, and perform the duties of life together as
becomes Christians, under Thy heavenly guidance and protection; through our Lord Jesus Christ. AMEN.

The Intent

MINISTER: _____, will you have this woman/man to be your wife/
husband, and will you pledge your troth to her/him, in all
love and honor, in all duty and service, in all faith and tenderness, to live with her/him and cherish her/him according
to the ordinance of God, in the holy bond of marriage?

GROOM/BRIDE: I will.

The Vows

GROOM/BRIDE *(repeat after Minister):* I, _____, take you to be my
wedded wife/husband, and I do promise and covenant,
before God and these witnesses, to be your loving and
faithful wife/husband, in plenty and in want, in joy and
in sorrow, in sickness and in health, as long as we both
shall live.

The Ring

MINISTER: Bless, O Lord, this ring, that he who gives it and she who
wears it may abide in Thy peace, and continue in Thy favor,
unto their life's end. AMEN.

GROOM: This ring I give you, in token and pledge, of our constant faith, and abiding love.

or:

With this ring I thee wed, in the name of the Father, and of the Son, and of the Holy Spirit. AMEN.

If a second ring is provided, a similar order shall be followed, the woman saying the same words after the Minister.

MINISTER: Let us pray. Most merciful and gracious God, of Whom the whole family in heaven and earth is named: Bestow upon these Thy servants the seal of Thine approval, and Thy Fatherly benediction; granting unto them grace to fulfill, with pure and steadfast affection, the vow and covenant between them made. Guide them together, we beseech Thee, in the way of righteousness and peace, that, loving and serving Thee, with one heart and mind, all the days of their lives, they may be abundantly enriched with the tokens of Thine everlasting favor, in Jesus Christ our Lord. AMEN.

Our Father, Who art in heaven,
Hallowed be Thy Name.
Thy kingdom come,
Thy will be done,
On earth as it is in heaven.

Give us this day our daily bread.
And forgive us our debts,
As we forgive our debtors.

And lead us not into temptation,
But deliver us from evil.
For Thine is the kingdom, and the power,
And the glory, forever. AMEN.

By the authority committed to me as a Minister of the Church of Christ, I declare that _____ and _____ are now husband and wife, according to the ordinance of God, and the law of the State; in the Name of the Father, and of the Son, and of the Holy Spirit. AMEN.

Husband and Wife join their right hands.

MINISTER: Whom therefore God hath joined together, let no man put asunder.

Benediction

Bride and Groom may kneel to receive this Benediction.

MINISTER: The Lord bless you, and keep you. The Lord make His face to shine upon you, and be gracious unto you. The Lord lift

up His countenance upon you, and give you peace, both now
and in the life everlasting. AMEN.

or:

God the Father, God the Son, God the Holy Spirit, bless, preserve, and keep you; the Lord mercifully with His favor look
upon you, and fill you with all spiritual benediction and
grace; that you may so live together in this life that in the
world to come you may have life everlasting. AMEN.

A METHODIST MARRIAGE SERVICE

MINISTER: Friends: We are gathered in the Church to celebrate and
praise God for the union of _____ and _____ in marriage. The bond and union of marriage were ordained by
God, Who created us male and female for each other. The
Apostle Paul announced that where Christ is present, there
is surely equality as well as unity. With His presence and
power, Jesus graced a wedding at Cana of Galilee. _____
and _____ have come here to join in marriage.

MINISTER *to Bride and Groom:* Christ calls you into union with Him and
with one another. I ask you now, in the presence of God and
this congregation, to declare your intent. Will you have this
man/woman to be your husband/ wife, to live together in a
holy marriage? Will you love him/her, comfort him/her,
honor and keep him/her in sickness and in health, and forsaking all others, be faithful to him/her as long as you both
shall live?

BRIDE/GROOM: I will.

MINISTER: Let us pray.
God of all peoples:
We rejoice in Your life in the midst of our lives.
You are the true light illumining everyone.
You show us the way, the truth, and the life.
You love us even when we are unfaithful.
You sustain us with Your Holy Spirit.
We praise You for Your presence with us,
And especially in this act of solemn covenant.
Through Jesus Christ our Lord. AMEN.

*One or more passages from the Scriptures may be read. Here are suggested
selections of Scripture readings.*

• *Psalms:* 23, 33 (sel.), 34, 37, 67, 103 (sel.), 112, 121, 127, 128, 145
(sel.), 148 (sel.)

- *Old Testament:*
  - Genesis 1:26-31; 2:18-25
  - Song of Solomon 1:15-16a; 2:2-3a,8-14,16a; 4:1a,9-10; 5:10,15b-16; 6:3a; 8:6-7
  - Isaiah 54:5-8
  - Jeremiah 31:31-34
  - Hosea 2:16-23
- *New Testament*
  - Matthew 5:1-10,13-16; 7:21,24-29; 19:3-6; 22:35-40
  - Mark 10:6-9,13-16
  - John 2:1-11; 15:9-16
  - Romans 12:1-2,9-18
  - Revelation 19:1,5-9a
  - I Corinthians 6:15-20; 12:31-13:8a; 13
  - Ephesians 3:14-21;5:2a,21-33
  - Colossians 3:12-17
  - I Peter 3:1-9
  - I John 3:18-24; 4:7-16
- *Apocrypha*
  - Tobit 8:5-10

Following the reading(s) from the Scriptures, the Minister blesses the Bride and Groom.

MINISTER: Let us pray.
Gracious God:
bless this man and woman
who come now to join in marriage
that they may give their vows to each other
in the strength and spirit of Your steadfast love.
Let the promise of Your word
root and grow in their lives.
Grant them vision and hope
to persevere in trust and friendship all their days.
Keep ever before them the need of the world.
By your grace
enable them to be true disciples of Jesus Christ,
in Whose Name we pray. AMEN.

The Marriage

BRIDE AND GROOM *face each other and join hands:* In the Name of God, I, _____, take you, _____, to be my husband/wife, to have and to hold from this day forward, for better for worse, for richer for poorer, in sickness and in health, to love and to cherish, until we are parted by death. This is my solemn vow.

The Exchange of Rings

MINISTER: Bless, O Lord, these rings, that they who wear them may then live in Your peace, and continue in Your favor all the days of their life, through Jesus Christ our Lord. AMEN.

BRIDE/GROOM: _____, I give you this ring as a sign of my vow, and with all that I am, and all that I have, I honor you.

Bride and Groom join hands.

MINISTER *to Bride and Groom:* You have declared your consent and vows before God and this congregation. May God confirm your covenant, and fill you both with grace.

MINISTER *to Congregation:* Now that _____ and _____ have given themselves to each other by solemn vows, with the joining of hands and the giving of rings, I announce to you that they are husband and wife in the Name of the Father, and of the Son, and of the Holy Spirit. Those whom God has joined together, let no one separate.

CONGREGATION: AMEN.

The service may continue with a service of thanksgiving and Lord's Prayer, holy communion, or the Agape Meal (Love Feast).

Dismissal with Blessing and the Peace

The minister blesses the new couple, and then the entire congregation. The couple and minister(s) may greet each other, after which greetings may be exchanged throughout the congregation. A hymn may be sung or other instrumental music may be played as the congregation leaves.

A CONTEMPORARY MARRIAGE SERVICE

MINISTER: Let us worship God.

There was a marriage at Cana in Galilee; Jesus was invited to the marriage, with His disciples.

Friends: Marriage is established by God. In marriage a man and a woman willingly bind themselves together in love, and become one, even as Christ is one with the Church, His body.

CONGREGATION: Let marriage be held in honor among all.

All may join in a hymn of praise and the following prayer.

MINISTER: Let us confess our sin before God.

CONGREGATION: Almighty God, our Father: You created us for life together. We confess that we have turned from Your will. We have not loved one another as You commanded. We have been quick to claim our own rights and careless of the rights of others. We have taken much and given little. Forgive our disobedience, O God, and strengthen us in love, so that we may serve You as a faithful people, and love together in Your joy; through Jesus Christ our Lord. AMEN.

MINISTER: Hear and believe the good news of the gospel.
Nothing can separate us from the love of God in Christ Jesus our Lord!

CONGREGATION: In Jesus Christ, we are forgiven.

The people may stand to sing a doxology, or some other appropriate response to the good mercy of God. The minister may offer a Prayer for Illumination. Before the reading of the Old Testament lesson, the minister shall say:

MINISTER: The lesson is ... . Listen for the Word of God.

The Gloria Patri, or some other response, may be sung. Before the reading of the New Testament lesson, the minister shall say:

MINISTER: The lesson is ... . Listen for the Word of God.

The minister may deliver a brief sermon on the lessons from Scripture, concluding with an Ascription of Praise.

MINISTER *to Bride and Groom:* _____ and _____, you have come together according to God's wonderful plan for Creation. Now, before these people, say your vows to each other.

Let the groom and the bride stand before the people, facing each other.

MINISTER: Be subject to one another out of reverence for Christ.

GROOM *to Bride:* _____, I promise with God's help to be your faithful husband, to love and serve you as Christ commands, as long as we both shall live.

BRIDE *to Groom:* _____, I promise with God's help to be your faithful wife, to love and serve you as Christ commands, as long as we both shall live.

A ring, or rings, may be given.

BRIDE/GROOM: I give you this ring as a sign of my promise.

MINISTER: As God's picked representatives of the new humanity, purified and beloved of God Himself, be merciful in action, kindly in heart, humble in mind. Accept life, and be most patient and tolerant with one another. Forgive as freely as the Lord has forgiven you. And, above everything else, be truly loving. Let the peace of Christ rule in your hearts, remembering that as members of the one body you are called to live in harmony, and never forget to be thankful for what God has done for you.

61

or:

Love is slow to lose patience—it looks for a way of being constructive. It is not possessive: It is neither anxious to impress nor does it cherish inflated ideas of its own importance. Love has good manners and does not pursue selfish advantage. It is not touchy. It does not keep account of evil or gloat over the wickedness of other people. On the contrary, it is glad with all good men when truth prevails. Love knows no limit to its endurance, no end to its trust, no fading of its hope; it can outlast anything. It still stands when all else has fallen.

MINISTER: Praise the Lord.

CONGREGATION: The Lord's Name be praised.

MINISTER: Lift up your hearts.

CONGREGATION: We lift them to the Lord.

MINISTER: Let us pray. Eternal God: Without your grace no promise is sure. Strengthen _____ and _____ with the gift of Your Spirit, so they may fulfill the vows they have taken. Keep them faithful to each other and to You. Fill them with such love and joy that they may build a home where no one is a stranger. And guide them by Your word to serve You all the days of their lives; through Jesus Christ our Lord, to Whom be honor and glory forever and ever. AMEN.

The Lord's Prayer shall be said. Bride and Groom then join hands.

MINISTER: _____ and _____, you are now husband and wife according to the witness of the holy catholic church, and the law of the State. Become one. Fulfill your promises. Love and serve the Lord.

CONGREGATION: What God has united, man must not divide.

Here may be sung a hymn of thanksgiving. Then, let the people be dismissed.

MINISTER: Glory be to Him Who can keep you from falling and bring you safe to His glorious presence, innocent and happy. To God, the only God, Who saves us through Jesus Christ our Lord, be the glory, majesty, authority, and power, which He had before time began, now and forever. AMEN.

or:

The grace of the Lord Jesus Christ, the love of God, and the fellowship of the Holy Spirit, be with you all. AMEN.

A UNITARIAN MARRIAGE SERVICE

The Unitarian Church does not offer a standard service, but leaves the composition of the service to each of its ministers. Consequently, among Unitarian-Universalists, one finds a variety of services, planned individually to reflect the creative talent of the officiating minister. The two services reproduced here were selected for their humanistic, rather than theological, references.

I

The Opening
The opening may be an informal welcome to guests as witnesses to the marriage or a literary statement.

Readings
Selections should represent the preferences of the bride, groom, and minister. Readings may be taken from the Testaments or classical or folk literature. A list of popular literary selections follows:

- Shakespeare, sonnet 116
- Elizabeth Barrett Browning, "How Do I Love Thee?"
- Kahlil Gibran, "Love One Another, but Make Not a Bond of Love..."
- James Russell Lowell, "True Love Is but a Humble, Lowborn Thing"
- John Ciardi, "Men Marry What They Need"
- e.e. cummings, "I carry your heart with me"
- Gerald M. Hopkins, "At the Wedding March"
- Carl Sandburg, "There Is a Place Where Love Begins"
- Philip Sidney, "Love's Tranquility"
- Stephen Sondheim, "Make of Our Hands, One Hand"

The Ceremony
MINISTER *to Congregation:* We come now to join _____ and _____ in marriage, reminding them that it is an estate desired and cherished by the peoples of all generations. With a love that will not falter and an abiding faith in one another, they will now make their vows one to another, as we, their witnesses and friends, will vow to support them as they begin the weaving of their lives in an endless togetherness.

MINISTER *to Bride and Groom:* _____, will you take _____ to be your husband/wife; love, honor and cherish him/her now and forevermore?

63

Weddings

BRIDE/GROOM: I will.

MINISTER: Repeat these words: I, _____, take you, _____, to be my husband/wife; to have and to hold from this day forward, for better for worse, for richer for poorer, in sickness and in health, to love and cherish always.

The Ring(s)

Groom and Bride give rings.

GROOM/BRIDE: With this ring, I wed you and pledge you my love now and forever.

or:

Be consecrated to me, with this ring, as my wife/husband in accordance with the faith of our loved ones.

The Wine Service

A single cup of wine is poured. Bride and Groom share the cup. A statement before and after the sharing of the cup is fittingly included in this service.

Conclusion

MINISTER: Foreasmuch as _____ and _____ have consented together in wedlock, and have so proclaimed before this company, and thereto have pledged themselves with word and symbol, I therefore pronounce them husband and wife.

Benediction

II

The Opening Words

MINISTER: "Love is the life of the soul. It is the harmony of the universe."—William Ellery Channing

"Love conquers all things; let us yield to love."—Virgil

We are gathered here together to unite this man and this woman in marriage, which is an institution founded in nature, ordained by the state, sanctioned by religion, and made honorable by the faithful keeping of good men and women in all ages.

This simple ceremony, this celebration, is the outward token of a sacred and inward union of hearts, a union created by loving purpose and kept by abiding will.

For what greater thing is there for two human souls than to feel that they are joined together to strengthen each other

in all labor, to minister to each other in all sorrow, to share
with each other all gladness, to be one with each other in the
silent unspeakable memories of the heart, and to convert
their private happiness into social blessing.

The Readings

MINISTER: In the words of the apostle Paul,

Love is patient and kind;
love is not jealous or boastful;
it is not arrogant or rude.
Love does not insist on its own way;
it is not irritable;
it does not rejoice at wrong,
but rejoices in the right.
Love bears all things, believes all things,
hopes all things, endures all things.

or:

In the words of the prophet Gibran,

Love one another, but make not a bond of love:
Let it rather be a moving sea between the shores of your
souls.
Fill each other's cup but drink not from one cup...
Give your hearts, but not into each other's keeping.
For only the hand of Life can contain your hearts.
And stand together, yet not too near together:
For the pillars of the temple stand apart,
And the oak tree and the cypress grow not in each other's
shadow...

MINISTER *to Bride and Groom:* _____, _____, it is in this spirit, I
know, that you two have come to be married. So let us proceed.

The Vows

MINISTER *to Bride and Groom:* _____, will you have _____ to be
your husband/wife, to live together in creating an abiding
marriage? Will you love and honor, comfort and cherish
him/her in sickness and in health, in sorrow and in joy, from
this day forward?

BRIDE/GROOM: I will.

The Rings

MINISTER: As a token of mutual fidelity and affection the ring(s) will
now be given and received.

The Prayer

MINISTER: The wedding is not over, it is just begun. Not once and forever, but again and again shall the mystery of two people,
together and in love, move one another and touch the world.
For marriage is not something said and done, but a promise,
whose fulfillment is acted out in time. Truth remains elusive,
death a secret, love a challenge; life goes on neither more
nor less incidentally than before, but one's hand is strengthened, one's way, brightened, and one's load, if not lightened,
is made easier to bear.

So for _____ and _____ we simply pray that the promises have a long and excellent fulfillment, that the company be good and the seasons joyous all along the way.
AMEN.

The Minister's Charge

MINISTER: _____, _____, I welcome you to the not always blissful,
but ever wondrous state of matrimony.

I have only this to ask of you.

May your hearts be as open as your minds are attentive and
discerning. May your lips sing forth the praise of every earthly good.

May your souls yearn for truth, to be sought in understanding. May your works be of love. May you stand where it shall
be right to have stood.

The Declaration of Marriage

MINISTER: And now, since you have pledged yourselves to each other
in the presence of this company, and have declared the
same by giving and receiving rings and by joining hands, I
do, by virtue of the authority vested in me, pronounce you,
_____ and _____, husband and wife.

The Benediction

MINISTER: And now may the love in your hearts and the greatness of
life's possibilities give you joy, and the assurance of your
friends' and families' good wishes give you peace and
strength. AMEN.

A FRIENDS MARRIAGE SERVICE

For the Religious Society of Friends, marriage is a binding relationship entered into in the presence of God and of witnessing friends.

The marriage takes place within a Meeting for Worship. Bride and Groom enter the Meeting and are seated at the front of the room. During the period of worship they rise, join hands, and make their promises to one another. They may use the following or similar words:

> In the presence of God and these our Friends, I take thee, _____,
> to be my wife/husband, promising with Divine assistance to be
> unto thee a loving and faithful wife/husband as long as we both
> shall live.

Friends do not require the presentation or exchange of rings. In conformity with custom, however, rings are often included.

After the vows are said and rings exchanged, the couple is seated. The marriage certificate is brought to them for their signatures. The certificate is then read aloud by someone chosen by the couple. The Meeting for Worship continues with silent prayer, meditation, and spoken messages.

The person who closes the Meeting arranges for the wedding party to withdraw. The congregation then, one by one, signs the certificate as witnesses to the marriage. The legal requirements are completed by a committee appointed by the Meeting.

It is interesting to note that, in giving themselves to each other, the custom of a bride being given away is eliminated. As no one officiates at the service, no one pronounces the bride and groom to be husband and wife. Friends believe that only God can create a union and give it significance.

The Roman Catholic Wedding

For the Roman Catholic, marriage is a sacrament, a visible sign of God's invisible grace and of His presence in the lives of those who submit to His word and His will. The wedding service is an act of holiness manifest in its words, symbols, and procedures. Married Christians, by way of the sacrament of marriage, share in the mystery of that love which exists between Christ and His Church. The actual marriage takes place in the covenant, the consent which each partner bestows upon the other and which constitutes the central theme of the marriage service. The guests are called upon to witness the sacrament; to worship with the bride and groom; and with them and their families, celebrate the benediction of marriage.

The wedding, in accordance with the Constitution on the Sacred Liturgy, takes place during a Mass held especially for the wedding. Under certain circumstances, a wedding may take place outside Mass, and a different rite is used.

Catholic wedding services are held during the day, scheduled before six o'clock. Weddings are not planned for Holy Thursday, Good Friday, or Holy Saturday, nor are weddings scheduled for those hours when Mass is read for the congregation.

The church is the appropriate setting for a wedding because it is a place sanctified by communal worhship and the place where the sacrament of marriage is more significantly symbolized. The wedding usually takes place in the parish church of the bride's family. If the couple prefers, they may be married in the church of the groom's family. For other churches or chapels, the permission of the bride's pastor is required. (In the New York diocese, permission can now be given for the ceremony to be conducted in a place other than a church or chapel. In this case, the priest must investigate the place

68

and certify that "the place chosen is a suitable one allowing for a dignified ceremony.")

PREMARITAL GUIDANCE

When plans get underway for a wedding, the Church makes certain requests of the bride and groom to help the couple with their spiritual preparation. Initially, the Church requests the presentation of (1) a baptismal certificate issued within six months of the wedding date, (2) a record of Confirmation, and (3) a letter of free state issued by the parishes of both parties. In addition, the prospective bride and groom participate in a prematrimonial investigation (PMI) in the presence of a priest. The couple answer questions to make certain that they plan to enter marriage freely and that they fully consent to one another. The priest may question the couple about their religious education, their respective communal and professional involvements, and the manner in which they plan to relate to one another in terms of their interests.

Young couples (often under the age of 24) are required to participate in a series of Pre-Cana, or premarital, conferences. Although older couples are not required to attend such sessions, it is recommended that they do so. The conferences deal with such subjects as communication in marriage, mature sexuality, and the sacrament of marriage. There are additional programs offered in various dioceses.

The "Engaged Encounter" is a weekend program for engaged couples. Small groups of engaged couples meet under the leadership of trained teams of married couples and priests. The engaged couples investigate, in a dialogue setting, their attitudes toward and expectations of each other regarding marriage, family, sexuality, the Church and society.

"Engage-Ment" is a one-day marriage program that affords bride and groom an opportunity to conduct an extensive examination of their ideals, goals, and desires with regard to the sacrament of marriage. The techniques used are similar to those of the weekend encounter.

"Evenings for the Engaged" is an in-home experience of six evenings, in which the engaged couple is matched with a married couple and a priest who share with them their knowledge of and experience in the sacrament of marriage. This parish-based program is set in the home of the married couple. "Evenings" is designed to bring engaged couples to a fuller awareness of what married life is from practical, human, and spiritual points of view.

WEDDING CUSTOMS

When a wedding is scheduled, banns (an announcement of the forthcoming marriage) may be read at a church service on three successive Sundays before the marriage. More commonly, however, the announcement appears in successive issues of the church bulletin. The priest may choose to dispense with the announcement.

A time should be established with the priest for a wedding rehearsal. To make the rehearsal a part of the total wedding experience, the couple may plan to attend an evening Mass, have their rehearsal, and then, with the wedding party, share in a prenuptial meal. Since it is customary for the bride's family to plan for the wedding and its celebration, the groom's family may make arrangements for the rehearsal evening.

Although religion is a spiritual experience, places of worship are institutions that require financial support. Therefore, fees or offerings may be suggested, or requested, for the use of church facilities for a wedding. If such a request poses a problem for the parishioner, the Church may adjust the fees accordingly.

The bride and groom are expected to present gifts to altar boys and church attendants. In addition, a couple who want to have an organist or vocalist at the wedding service is responsible for their fees. The couple may also wish to prepare a program for their guests. The printed piece could include the order of the service; the text of the readings, hymns, and responses to be sung and recited by the witnesses (guests); the names of the participants in the wedding service and ceremony; and a personal message from the bride and groom.

Churches permit floral decorations for a wedding with the understanding that the flowers remain in the church. There is a practice among some of transposing flowers from church to the place or hall where the celebration takes place, thus reducing the cost of flowers for wedding and celebration. However, the Catholic Church feels that flowers that are part of the wedding scene take on the spirit of the sacrament and should remain in the church for others to share.

There is an old tradition of throwing rice at the bride and groom at the conclusion of the marriage service to wish the couple good luck. In recent years, the Church and insurance companies have found the practice potentially dangerous. People have been known to slip on rice kernels or to have one stray piece scratch an eye. Because accidents can certainly dampen everyone's spirits, many churches have abandoned the practice of throwing rice. Some churches require a "deposit guarantee" that no rice will be thrown.

When a marriage takes place between two Catholics of mixed rites, it is the rite of the groom that determines the service to be used. The power to transfer rites from the groom's church to that of the bride rests with the Church.

THE WEDDING SERVICE

The wedding service may include most or all of these parts. Detailed explanations of each follow. (During Mass, the Nuptial Blessing follows the Lord's Prayer.)

1. **Entrance**
   Greeting to the Bride, Groom, and Witnesses
   Opening Prayer
2. **Liturgy of the Word**
   Old Testament Reading
   Responsorial Psalm
   New Testament Reading
   Gospel Acclamation ("Alleluia")
   Gospel Reading
3. **Homily**
4. **Rite of Marriage**
   Consent/Vows
   Exchange of Rings
   The Prayer of the Faithful
5. **Liturgy of the Eucharist**
6. **The Lord's Prayer**
7. **Nuptial Blessing**
8. **Conclusion**
   Blessing

The **entrance** may take the form of a procession in which the priest and ministers meet and greet the bride and groom at the entrance to the church and then lead them and their attendants to the altar; or the priest and ministers proceed to the altar to receive the bride, groom, and their attendants.

71

The **greeting** is usually an informal statement of welcome directed first to the bride and groom and then to their guests, followed by an **opening prayer.** Below is a sample opening prayer.

> Father,
> when You created mankind,
> You willed that man and wife should be one.
> Bind _____ and _____
> in the loving union of marriage
> and make their love fruitful
> so that they may be living witnesses
> to Your Divine love in the world.
> We ask You this
> through our Lord Jesus Christ, Your Son,
> Who lives and reigns with You and the Holy Spirit,
> one God, forever and ever.

The **liturgy of the word** includes readings from the **Old** and **New Testaments, a responsorial psalm, verse before the Gospel,** and a **Gospel reading.**

The bride and groom may wish to review with the priest the available lists of Testament and Gospel readings and select those they want to include in their service. The selections may be read by the priest or by honored members of the wedding party. It is appropriate to have the fathers of the bride and groom read the Testament selections. When guests are chosen for readings, it is advisable that they study the text, making certain they are familiar with the words, especially those that are not commonly used. Below is a suggested list of readings.

- *Old Testament*
  - Genesis 1:27 (The creation of man and woman)
  - Genesis 2:21 (The creation of woman)
  - Genesis 24:28 (The meeting of Isaac and Rebekah)
  - Ruth 1:16 (Ruth's determination)
  - Tobit 8:4 (The marriage of Tobias and Sarah)
  - Song of Songs 2:8-10,14,16; 8:6 (Love is as strong as death)
  - Proverbs 31:10 (A woman of valor)
- *New Testament*
  - Romans 8:31-35,37-39 (The love of Christ)
  - Romans 12:1-2,9-18 (The life of a Christian)
  - I Corinthians 13:1-8 (Love never fails)

- Ephesians 5:2,21-33 (The mystery of marriage)
- Colossians 3:12 (Live in love and thanksgiving)
- I Peter 3:1-9 (Peace and harmony in the family)
- I John 3:18-24 (Love, real and active)
- I John 4:7-12 (God is love)
- Revelation 19:1,5-9 (Marriage of the lamb)
- Matthew 5:1-12 (The Beatitudes)
- Matthew 5:13-16 (Light of the world)
- Matthew 7:21,24-29 (House built upon a rock)
- Matthew 19:3-6 (God has united, man must not divide)
- Matthew 22:35-40 (The commandment of love)
- John 2:1-11 (Marriage feast of Cana)
- John 15:9-12 (Remain in my love)
- John 15:12-16 (Love one another)
- John 17:20-26 (That they may be one)

The **homily** or sermon elaborates on the marriage theme. If the priest knows the couple well, he may interlace his homily with personal references.

The language of the **rite of marriage** varies. Here is one sample.

All stand.

PRIEST *to Bride and Groom:* My dear friends, you have come together in this church so that the Lord may seal and strengthen your love in the presence of the Church's minister and this community. Christ abundantly blesses this love. He has already consecrated you in baptism and now He enriches and strengthens you by a special sacrament so that you may assume the duties of marriage in mutual and lasting fidelity. And so, in the presence of the Church, I ask you to state your intentions.

The priest then questions them.

PRIEST: Have you, _____ and _____, come here freely and without reservation to give yourselves to each other in marriage?

BRIDE/GROOM: I have.

PRIEST: Will you love and honor each other as husband and wife for the rest of your lives?

BRIDE/GROOM: I will.

PRIEST: Will you accept children lovingly from God and bring them up according to the law of Christ and His Church?

BRIDE/GROOM: I will.

The priest invites the couple to declare their **consent.**

Weddings

PRIEST: Since it is your intention to enter into marriage, join your right hands, and declare your consent before God and His Church.

Bride and Groom join right hands.

GROOM/BRIDE: I, _____, take you, _____, for my lawful wife/husband, to have and to hold, from this day forward, for better for worse, for richer for poorer, in sickness and health, until death do us part.

or:

PRIEST: If it be your intention to enter into marriage, join your right hands and declare your consent before God and His Church.

BRIDE/GROOM: I, _____, take you, _____, to be my husband/wife. I promise to be true to you in good times and in bad, in sickness and in health. I will love and honor you all the days of my life.

PRIEST: You have declared your consent before the Church. May the Lord in His goodness strengthen your consent and fill you both with His blessings. What God has joined, men must not divide.

There are various wordings for the **exchange of rings.** Here are several.

PRIEST: May the Lord bless these rings
which you give to each other
as the sign of your love and fidelity.

or:

Lord bless these rings which we bless in Your Name.
Grant that those who wear them
may always have a deep faith in each other.
May they do Your will
and always live together.
We ask this through Christ our Lord.

or:

Lord,
bless and consecrate _____ and _____
in their love for each other.
May these rings be a symbol
of true faith in each other,
and always remind them of their love
through Christ our Lord.

The Groom places a ring on the third finger, left hand, of the Bride.

GROOM/BRIDE: _____, take this ring as a sign of my love and my fidelity. In the name of the Father, and of the Son, and of the Holy Spirit.

The Bride, in turn, places a ring on the fourth finger, left hand, of the Groom, and speaks the same words.

The **prayer of the faithful** follows. (A personal prayer can be included here if the bride and groom so desire.)

During Mass, the **Liturgy of the Eucharist** is said at this time. (Those chosen to bring gifts of wine and bread to the altar carry out their role at this point and the Liturgy of the Eucharist begins.)

The priest then offers the **Nuptial Blessing.**

The priest faces the Bride and Bridegroom. They join hands.

> PRIEST: My dear friends, let us turn to the Lord and pray
> that He will bless with His grace this woman
> now married in Christ to this man
> and that through the sacrament of the body and blood of Christ,
> He will unite in love the couple He has joined in this holy bond.

All pray silently for a short while. Then the priest extends his hands and continues:

> Father, by Your power You have made everything out of nothing.
> In the beginning You created the universe
> and made mankind in Your own likeness.
> You gave man the constant help of woman
> so that man and woman should no longer be two, but one flesh,
> and You teach us that what You have united
> may never be divided.

or:

> Father, You have made the union of man and wife so holy a mystery
> that it symbolizes the marriage of Christ and His Church.

or:

> Father, by Your plan man and woman are united,
> and married life has been established
> as the one blessing that was not forfeited by original sin
> or washed away in the flood.
> Look with love upon this woman, Your daughter,
> now joined to her husband in marriage.
> She asks Your blessing.
> Give her the grace of love and peace.
> May she always follow the example of the holy women
> whose praises are sung in the Scriptures.

May her husband put his trust in her
and recognize that she is his equal
and the heir with him to the life of grace.
May he always honor her and love her
as Christ loves His bride, the Church.

Father, keep them always true to Your commandments.
Keep them faithful in marriage
and let them be living examples of Christian life.

Give them the strength which comes from the Gospel
so that they may be witnesses of Christ to others.
Bless them with children
and help them to be good parents.
May they live to see their children's children.
And, after a happy old age,
grant them fullness of life with the saints
in the Kingdom of Heaven.

We ask this through Christ our Lord. AMEN.

Other forms of the nuptial blessing follow.

PRIEST: Let us pray to the Lord for _____ and _____,
who come to God's altar at the beginning of their married life
so that they may always be united in love for each other
as they now share in the body and blood of Christ.

All pray silently for a short while. Then the priest extends his hands and continues.

Holy Father, You created mankind in Your own image
and made man and woman to be joined as husband and wife
in union of body and heart
and so fulfill their mission in this world.

or:

Father, to reveal the plan of Your love,
You made the union of husband and wife
an image of the covenant between You and Your people.
In the fulfillment of this sacrament,
the marriage of Christian man and woman
is a sign of the marriage between Christ and the Church.
Father, stretch out Your hand, and bless _____ and _____.

Lord, grant that as they begin to live this sacrament
they may share with each other the gifts of Your love
and become one in heart and mind,

as witnesses to Your presence in their marriage.
Help them to create a home together
and give them children to be formed by the gospel
and to have a place in Your family.

Give Your blessings to _____, Your daughter,
so that she may be a good wife and mother,
caring for the home,
faithful in love for her husband,
generous and kind.

Give Your blessings to _____, Your son,
so that he may be a faithful husband
and a good father.

Father, grant that as they come together to Your table on
    earth,
so they may one day have the joy of sharing Your feast in
    heaven.

We ask this through Christ our Lord.
AMEN.

or:

My dear friends, let us ask God
for His continued blessings upon this bridegroom and his
    bride.

All pray silently for a while. Then the priest extends his hands and continues.

PRIEST: Holy Father, Creator of the universe
Maker of man and woman in Your own likeness,
Source of blessing for married life,
we humbly pray to You for this woman,
who today is united with her husband in this sacrament of
    marriage.

May Your fullest blessing come upon her and her husband
so that they may together rejoice in Your gift of married love
and enrich Your Church with their children.

Lord, may they both praise You when they are happy
and turn to You in their sorrows.
May they be glad that You help them in their work
and know that You are with them in their need.
May they pray to You in the community of the Church,
and be Your witnesses in the world.
May they reach old age in the company of their friends,
and come at last to the Kingdom of Heaven.

We ask this through Christ our Lord.
AMEN.

The **conclusion** of a wedding without Mass is the **Lord's Prayer** and a **Blessing.** At a Mass, the service ends with a **Blessing** and **Dismissal.**

PRIEST: God the eternal Father keep you in love with each other,
so that the peace of Christ may stay with you
and be always in your home.
AMEN.

May your children bless you,
your friends console you,
and all men live in peace with you.
AMEN.

May you always bear witness to the love of God in this world
so that the afflicted and the needy
will find in you generous friends,
and welcome you into the joys of heaven.
AMEN.

And may almighty God bless you all,
the Father, and the Son, and the Holy Spirit.
AMEN.

or:

May God, the almighty Father,
give you His joy
and bless you in your children.
AMEN.

May the only Son of God have mercy on you
and help you in good times and in bad.
AMEN.

May the Holy Spirit of God
always fill your hearts with His love.
AMEN.

And may almightly God bless you all,
the Father, and the Son, and the Holy Spirit.
AMEN.

or:

May the Lord Jesus, Who was a guest at the wedding in Cana,
bless you and your families and friends.
AMEN.

May Jesus, Who loved His Church to the end,
always fill your hearts with His love.

AMEN.

May He grant that, as you believe in His resurrection,
so may you wait for Him in joy and hope.

AMEN.

And may almighty God bless you all,
the Father, and the Son, and the Holy Spirit.

AMEN.

In the dioceses of the United States, the following form may be used.

PRIEST: May almighty God, with His Word of blessing, unite your hearts in the never-ending bond of pure love.

AMEN.

May your children bring you happiness, and may your generous love for them be returned to you, many times over.

AMEN.

May the peace of Christ live always in your hearts and in your home.

May you have true friends to stand by you, both in joy and in sorrow.

May you be ready and willing to help and comfort all who come to you in need.

And may the blessings promised to the compassionate be yours in abundance.

AMEN.

May you find happiness and satisfaction in your work.

May daily problems never cause you undue anxiety, nor the desire for earthly possessions dominate your lives.

But may your hearts' first desire be always the good things waiting for you in the life of heaven.

AMEN.

May the Lord bless you with many happy years together, so that you may enjoy the rewards of a good life.

And after you have served Him loyally in His kingdom on earth, may he welcome you to His eternal kingdom in heaven.

AMEN.

And may almighty God bless you all, the Father, and the Son, and the Holy Spirit.

AMEN.

WEDDING MUSIC

The Commission on Church Music of the Archdiocese of New York has published a statement entitled *Music for Weddings,* in which the following observations are made:

> The music of the wedding service should assist the assembled believers to express and share the gift of faith. This does not exclude songs from the popular idiom, especially those which can be seen as referring to the human-divine nature of love.

Examples of such songs are "Sabbath Prayer" from *Fiddler on the Roof* and "Wedding Song" recorded by Paul Stookey of Peter, Paul, and Mary.

The Commission makes these suggestions:

1. The bridal party may be ushered in with an entrance song sung by the assembled in place of a march.
2. In place of the traditional soloist, the singer may function as a leader of song and involve those present in the people's part of the Mass.
3. The Responsorial Psalm may be sung at a Wedding Mass.
4. The "Holy, Holy," "Memorial Acclamation," "Amen," and "Our Father" may be sung by the assembled.
5. If a Communion song is sung, it should not be to the Blessed Mother, but should reflect what is happening at the time. If a hymn to Mary is desired, at some other time, there are excellent Marian hymns. The four chant melodies are among the most beautiful.
6. Besides the organ and the recently introduced guitar, other instruments are approved for use at a wedding. The flute, harp, oboe, and trumpet are all quite effective in a wedding celebration.

Recommended music before the Processional includes:

- Bach, "Jesus bleibt meine Freude," Chorale from *Cantata 147*
- Purcell, *Keyboard Music*
- Bach, *Eight Little Preludes and Fugues for the Organ*
- World Library of Sacred Music, *All Around Bach, Book I*
- Concordia Music Publishing House, *Wedding Music, Part I*
- Schirmer Publishing Co., *Royal Fireworks Music*
- Handel, *Water Music*

Songs to use before or during weddings include:

- *The Lord's Prayer*
- Handel, *Wedding Hymn*

- Wetzer, *Bless Us, God of Loving*
- Schutz, *Wedding Song*
- Cassler, *Three Wedding Solos*
- Leopold, *Wedding Processional and Air*
- Roff, *Bless, O Lord, These Rings*
- Proulx, *Nuptial Blessing*
- Proulx, *Beloved, Let Us Love*
- Sister Germaine, *Love One Another*
- *In Love We Gather*
- *All the Earth Proclaim the Lord*
- *Like Olive Branches*
- People's Mass Book, *Take Our Bread*
- World Library of Sacred Music, *Now Joined by God*
- *These Two*
- *Where Love and Charity Abide*
- *Psalm 127*
- Worship (Hymn Book), *May the Grace of Christ*
- *Love Divine, All Love Excelling*
- *Lord, May Their Lives*
- *O Perfect Love*

The Jewish Wedding

I n the Jewish experience, marriage is a *mitzvah*, a requirement for the fulfillment of one's destiny. The wedding service is an act of *Kiddushin*, sanctification. A man and a woman "find favor in each other's eyes" and are set apart from all others for the purpose of urging each other on toward the fulfillment of their respective promises to the universe.

The wedding service, in its various forms, represents the blending of legal and religious practices. It is also influenced by the folk custom of the peoples of the many lands in which the Jewish people have lived.

In Jewish life, there are three major religious points of view: Orthodox, Conservative, and Reform (or Liberal). Each interprets the nature and purpose of Jewish existence differently, manifest in the requirements and procedures for the wedding service. These variations are noted below.

THE TIME FOR A WEDDING

A wedding is not planned for a Sabbath, a holy day, a festival, or other special times during the year.

In contemporary practice, Saturday evening is a choice time for a wedding. A question arises as to when on the Sabbath a service may be performed. In the Orthodox tradition, this is determined by the *sheki'ah*, the time when the Sabbath day has departed and the week has begun. "Departure time" calendars are available.

In Liberal tradition, a time generally considered to be the onset of evening is looked upon as a proper time for a Saturday wedding. This time may vary from place to place, rabbi to rabbi.

There is a significant difference between the Orthodox and Liberal communities in the observance of the holy days, particularly the festivals. Orthodoxy prohibits weddings on the second day of any festival, while the Liberal tradition permits them. The two-day festivals are Passover, Shavu'ot, and Sukkot. This difference also pertains to the second day of Rosh ha-Shanah.

Periods during the year when Orthodox tradition forbids marriage ceremonies are the seven weeks beginning with Passover and concluding with the festival of Shavu'ot (there are excepted days during this period, which vary within the Orthodox tradition) and a period corresponding to the June–July season, beginning with the 17th day of the Hebrew month of Tammuz and ending with the 9th day of the month of Av. Liberal rabbis do not follow these restrictions, except for the 9th day of Av, which for some rabbis is a day of abstention. In recent times, Yom ha-Sho'ah, Holocaust Day, has been listed as a forbidden day.

How does one approach these restrictions in the planning of a wedding? Those establishing the time for a wedding are advised to reflect upon the attitudes and practices of their guests. If even a few guests will not attend the wedding, or if they might attend and feel uncomfortable, then obviously the restrictions should be adhered to. If the guests will not find the traditional restrictions disturbing, a wedding could be properly scheduled during a time restricted for some, but not for all traditions.

THE SYMBOLS OF THE WEDDING SERVICE

The symbols of the wedding service are the canopy, a cup of wine (or two), the ring(s), the *Ketubah,* the bride's veil, the marriage altar, and the breaking of a glass.

The Canopy *(Chuppah)*

The canopy, or *Chuppah,* is very much a part of a Jewish wedding. In the language of marriage, the people speak of "bringing a child to the *Chuppah.*" The canopy is the "bower" to which bride and groom retire to taste the sweetness of their love. Aside from traditional references to this practice, it is an attractive element. It sets bride and groom apart from all others, dramatizing the concept of *Kiddushin* as it historically describes a wedding.

Some synagogues have a permanent *Chuppah.* Generally it is a covering under which bride and groom stand during the service. The

83

Chuppah may be artistically designed or simply a frame adorned with flowers. A popular ancient practice was to use a large prayer shawl held over the head of bride and groom.

A *Chuppah* can be easily made. Needed is a stretch of cloth, as colorful and attractive as suits the taste of those who select the material, sixty inches in length and width (a standard size), four dowels, and a few tacks. The material might be hemmed to give it a finished look. It is then placed over the dowels, each dowel at one corner of the material, less three or four inches for an overhang, and tacked to the dowel. Dowels can be obtained at most lumberyards. They come in a variety of sizes. Best are the eight-foot dowels, which should be cut down to six foot, or some inches more if the couple requires the height. Long dowels are preferable. Those who will hold the *Chuppah* must hold the dowels to the floor. A short dowel tires the arm and causes the *Chuppah* to sail distractingly up and back across the heads of bride and groom. There is also available a metal base measuring approximately ten inches square, with a protrusion that holds a length of two-inch by two-inch lumber, obtainable at any lumberyard in varying lengths. The advantage of this base is that the canopy can stand without being held.

The Ring(s)

The ring, though not required, is a common and dramatic element in wedding services. Originally, when legal interests were dominant, an object of value was used by the groom to "acquire" the bride. In time, this took the form of a ring. The groom places a ring upon the finger of his bride while saying, "Be sanctified to me, with this ring, in accordance with the laws of Moses and Israel."

By tradition, the ring is no more than a simple band, and there is a good reason for it. In the closed communities in which Jews lived, the most disturbing of social forces was the competitive need to demonstrate affluence or attainment. A wedding ceremony is just one of those occasions when a family may choose to make a statement concerning status. In the small, closed community, such representations evoked envy and embarrassment on the part of those who would, if they could, send their children off "in clouds of glory." The sages of Judaism, sensitive to this condition, sought to reduce social differences, especially with regard to a wedding, and ordered that the wedding ring be no more than a simple band.

The contemporary service often involves an exchange of rings. The groom places a ring upon the finger of the bride and then the bride places a ring on the finger of her groom. This practice is not permitted in the Orthodox service, which follows the older tradition in which the ring is used to "acquire" the bride. In the Conservative service, a different set of words is used by groom and bride in the exchange of the rings.

For Jewish tradition, the ring finger is the fourth finger of the right hand, differing from other American traditions. Often, following a service, a bride will remove the ring from the "finger of tradition" and place it upon another. Since the ceremony of the placing of the ring gives to both ring and finger a mystical quality, it is advised that, if the bride prefers to wear her ring on a particular finger, the ring be placed upon that finger during the service.

The Veil

The story of the veil reaches back to the biblical account of the trials of Jacob, who was in love with his cousin Rachel. He asked his uncle, Laban, for her hand. Laban agreed to do so, but only in return for some years of Jacob's servitude. When Jacob had fulfilled his part of the bargain, he asked for Rachel. In response, his uncle Laban set a time for the wedding. "But behold, on the morrow Jacob discovered that it was Leah and not Rachel who had been given to him behind her veil."

To assure a groom that the bride he had bargained for is the bride he would get, there developed the practice of "Covering the Bride," which is still followed in some quarters. The groom and witnesses approach the bride prior to the wedding service, ascertain that she is the bride, and then take the veil and place it over her head. The officiant may recite the following:

> Our sister, be thou the mother of thousands of myriads.
> God make thee as Sarah, Rebekah, Rachel, and Leah.
> May the Lord bless thee and keep thee.
> May the Lord let His countenance shine upon thee, and be
>   gracious unto thee.
> May the Lord lift up His countenance upon thee, and give thee
>   peace.

At one time, the veil had a significance in the legal and social customs of society. Today, however, the veil is part of the wedding costume, retained for no other reason than its attractiveness. Consequently, the choice of veil will represent the bride's preferences.

In many weddings, it is lifted after the groom has tasted from the cup of wine. Often, the bride will have the veil returned to its place and it will not be lifted again until the conclusion of the service, when the groom embraces the bride. There is no required time for the lifting of the veil.

The Wine Service

Wine, a symbol of sanctification, is prominent in Jewish life-cycle and calendar observations and celebrations. With the wine, praise is given to God, "He who created the fruit of the vine." Bride and groom share the cup of wine, symbolizing a need and a desire to share in the spirit and the mystery of the creative process. Any wine that submits to the blessing "fruit of the vine" is acceptable for the service. The label "kosher" for wines is an improper designation. The juice of all grapes is, by its nature, kosher—acceptable to the Jewish catalogue of foods and liquors. At one time, some wines were excluded from Jewish use, not because of the wine itself, but because of the manner in which it was processed and bottled. There is a carry-over of the injunction into modern practice, with wines being designated kosher to signify that the process and bottling are acceptable.

The Cup

Any glass or cup may be used for the service. The selection of a particular cup, one used in sanctifying the family's life-cycle and calendar observances, adds to the spirit and intent of the wedding service. Because the bride and groom are establishing a new home, a new cup may be used. A "Loving Cup"—distinguished by its two handles which can be inscribed with the names of the bride and groom —is often used and serves as a wedding memento.

In some services two cups of wine are used, combining both the engagement and the wedding services. A cup of wine is used for each. (This practice is described below in the section on the wedding service.) Some rabbis conduct a single wedding service but retain the two cups, using one to symbolize the sweetness in the promise of marriage and the other, the bitterness that is in the nature of life. "As together you now drink from this cup, ... so may you find its joys doubly gladdening ... its bitterness sweetened."

The *Ketubah*

The *Ketubah* is a document recording the particulars of a marriage: date, place, and identification of bride and groom and their families, together with conditions pertaining to the marriage. Originally, this document was a legal instrument. The particulars recorded were designed to protect the bride in the event of a dissolution of the marriage. The *Ketubah* is written in Aramaic, the ancient vernacular of the Hebrews. In time, the text of the *Ketubah* was standardized; it has taken on a religious rather than legal significance. The *Ketubah* is traditionally read during the Orthodox wedding service and delivered to the bride.

Liberal (Reform) Judaism has omitted the *Ketubah,* finding the text irrelevant to the contemporary experience. Furthermore, since the state assumed the responsibility for sanctioning marriages, the *Ketubah* is only a rememberance of things past.

Still, many families today wish to have a *Ketubah* as a record noting the onset of the marriage in place of the card or certificate a rabbi might deliver to bride and groom. *Ketubot* with applicable text, fitting the contemporary understanding of the roles of marriage partners, are available. Many of them are artistically designed, reminiscent of an ancient and attractive tradition. The text of a *Ketubah* published by Emanuel Press and set in a series of lithographs reads as follows:

On the _____ day of the month of _____ in the year _____, corresponding to the traditional calendar year of _____, at _____, in the city of _____ and the State of _____, _____, the son of _____ and _____ of the family of _____, and _____, daughter of _____ and _____ of the family of _____, have entered into a covenant of marriage in accordance with the tradition of Judaism and have said, one to another, I will revere your person, and respect your aspirations.

I will share with you the love of my heart, the substance of my dreams, and the fruits of my labors, and I will now and forever urge you toward the recognition and the fulfillment of the promise that is within you, to the end that we might together make our lives purposeful and become together co-workers with God in the process of creation.

We give thanks to God Whose gift of love has brought us together and lifted us up above all others, to Him Who created joy and gladness, bride and groom, mirth and song, harmony, peace and companionship.

Praise be given to Him Who causes bride and groom to rejoice together. In promise and commitment, we here affix our names as we give them to each other.

Bride _____   Witness _____
Groom _____   Witness _____
Rabbi _____

The Text of the Traditional *Ketubah*

בְּ _____ בְּשַׁבָּת, _____ יוֹם (יָמִים) לְחֹדֶשׁ _____, שְׁנַת
חֲמֵשֶׁת אֲלָפִים וּשְׁבַע מֵאוֹת וְ _____ לִבְרִיאַת הָעוֹלָם, לְמִנְיָן שֶׁאָנוּ
מוֹנִין כָּאן, _____, בִּמְדִינַת אֲמֶרִיקָה הַצְּפוֹנִית, אֵיךְ הֶחָתָן, ר'
_____ בֶּן ר' _____ (הַכֹּהֵן), אָמַר לָהּ לַהֲדָא בְּתוּלְתָא,
בַּת ר' _____, הֱוֵי לִי לְאִנְתּוּ כְּדַת מֹשֶׁה וְיִשְׂרָאֵל, וַאֲנָא אֶפְלַח וְאוֹקִיר
וְאֵיזוֹן וַאֲפַרְנֵס יָתִיכִי (לִיכִי) כְּהִלְכוֹת גּוּבְרִין יְהוּדָאִין דְּפָלְחִין וּמוֹקְרִין
וְזָנִין וּמְפַרְנְסִין לִנְשֵׁיהוֹן בְּקוּשְׁטָא. וְיָהֵבְנָא לִיכִי מֹהַר בְּתוּלַיְכִי כְּסַף זוּזֵי
מָאתָן דְּחָזֵי לִיכִי מִדְּאוֹרַיְתָא, וּמְזוֹנַיְכִי וּכְסוּתַיְכִי וְסִפּוּקַיְכִי, וּמֵיעַל
לְוָתַיְכִי כְּאוֹרַח כָּל אַרְעָא. וּצְבִיאַת מָרַת _____ בְּתוּלְתָא דָא וַהֲוַת לֵהּ
לְאִנְתּוּ, וְדֵין נְדוּנְיָא דְּהַנְעֲלַת לֵהּ מִבֵּי אֲבוּהָ בֵּין בְּכֶסֶף בֵּין בְּדְהַב בֵּין
בְּתַכְשִׁיטִין, בְּמָאנֵי דִלְבוּשָׁא, בְּשִׁמּוּשֵׁי דִירָה וּבְשִׁמּוּשֵׁי דְעַרְסָא, הַכֹּל
קִבֵּל עָלָיו ר' _____ חָתָן דְּנָן בְּמֵאָה זְקוּקִים כֶּסֶף צָרוּף. וְצָבִי ר'
_____ חָתָן דְּנָן וְהוֹסִיף לָהּ מִן דִּילֵהּ עוֹד מֵאָה זְקוּקִים כֶּסֶף צָרוּף
אֲחֵרִים כְּנֶגְדָּן, סַךְ הַכֹּל מָאתַיִם זְקוּקִים כֶּסֶף צָרוּף. וְכַךְ אָמַר ר' _____
חָתָן דְּנָן, אַחֲרָיוּת שְׁטַר כְּתוּבְתָּא דָא, נְדוּנְיָא דֵן וְתוֹסֶפְתָּא דָא קַבְּלִית
עֲלַי וְעַל יָרְתַי בַּתְרַאי לְהִתְפְּרַע מִכָּל שְׁפַר אֲרַג נִכְסִין וְקִנְיָנִין דְּאִית לִי
תְּחוֹת כָּל שְׁמַיָּא, דִּקְנַאי וּדְעָתִיד אֲנָא לְמִקְנָא, נִכְסִין דְּאִית לְהוֹן אַחֲרָיוּת
וּדְלֵית לְהוֹן אַחֲרָיוּת, כֻּלְּהוֹן יְהוֹן אַחֲרָאִין וְעַרְבָאִין לִפְרוֹעַ מִנְּהוֹן שְׁטַר
כְּתוּבְתָּא דָא, נְדוּנְיָא דֵן וְתוֹסֶפְתָּא דָא מִנַּאי, וַאֲפִילוּ מִן גְּלִימָא דְעַל
כַּתְפָּאי, בְּחַיֵּי וּבָתַר חַיַּי, מִן יוֹמָא דְנָן וּלְעָלַם. וְאַחֲרָיוּת שְׁטַר כְּתוּבְתָּא
דָא, נְדוּנְיָא דֵן וְתוֹסֶפְתָּא דָא, קַבֵּל עָלָיו ר' _____ חָתָן דְּנָן כְּחוֹמֶר
כָּל שְׁטָרֵי כְתוּבוֹת וְתוֹסֶפְתּוֹת דְּנָהֲגִין בִּבְנוֹת יִשְׂרָאֵל, הָעֲשׂוּיִין כְּתִקּוּן
חֲכָמֵינוּ זִכְרָם לִבְרָכָה; דְּלָא כְּאַסְמַכְתָּא וּדְלָא כְּטוֹפְסֵי דִשְׁטָרֵי. וְקָנֵינָא
מִן ר' _____ בֶּן _____ (הַכֹּהֵן) חָתָן דְּנָן לְמָרַת _____ בַּת ר'
_____ בְּתוּלְתָא דָא עַל כָּל מַה דְּכָתוּב וּמְפוֹרָשׁ לְעֵיל בְּמָאנָא דְכָשֵׁר
לְמִקְנָא בֵּהּ, וְהַכֹּל שָׁרִיר וְקַיָּם.
נְאוּם _____ בֶּן _____, עֵד. וּנְאוּם _____ בֶּן _____, עֵד.

Translation of the Text of the Traditional *Ketubah*

On the _____ day of the week, the _____ day of the
month _____, in the year Five Thousand, Seven Hundred
and _____ since the creation of the world, the era according
to which we are accustomed to reckon here in the city of
_____, _____, son of _____, surnamed _____, came
and said to this virgin, _____, daughter of _____, surnamed _____:

"Be my wife according to the law of Moses and Israel, and I
will cherish, honor, and support and maintain you in accordance with the custom of Jewish husbands who cherish, honor,

88

support and maintain their wives in truth. And I herewith make for you the settlement of virgins, two hundred silver *zuzim,* which belongs to you, according to the law of Moses and Israel; and your food, clothing and necessaries, according to the universal custom." And _____, this virgin, consented and became his wife. The wedding outfit that she brought to him from her father's house, in silver, gold, valuables, wearing apparel, house furniture, and bedclothes—all this _____, the said bridegroom, accepted in the sum of one hundred silver pieces.

_____, the bridegroom, added one hundred silver pieces of his own, to match hers, for a total of two hundred silver pieces. And thus said _____, the bridegroom:

"The responsibility of this marriage contract, of this wedding outfit, and of this additional sum, I take upon myself and my heirs after me, so that they shall be paid from the best part of my property and possession that I have beneath the whole heaven, that which I now possess or may hereafter acquire. All my property, real and personal, even the mantle on my shoulders, shall be mortgaged to secure the payment of this marriage contract, of the wedding outfit, and of the addition made thereto, during my lifetime and after my death, from the present day and forever."

_____, the bridegroom, has taken upon himself the responsibility of this marriage contract, of this wedding outfit, and of the addition made thereto, according to the restrictive usages of all marriage contracts and the additions thereto made for the daughters of Israel, in accordance with the institution of our sages of blessed memory. It is not to be regarded as a mere forfeiture without consideration or as a mere formula of a document.

We have followed the legal formality of symbolic delivery *(kinyan)* between _____, the son of _____, the bridegroom, and _____, the daughter of _____, this virgin, and we have used a garment legally fit for the purpose, to strengthen all that is stated above,

AND EVERTHING IS VALID AND CONFIRMED.

Attested to _____ (Witness) Attested to _____ (Witness)

The Text of the Conservative *Ketubah.* The text of the Conservative *Ketubah* parallels the Orthodox except that a number of lines have been added. The addition contains a statement that in the event the marriage fails and is dissolved under civil law, "husband and wife will invoke the authority of the *Beth Din* [Canonical Court] of the Rabbinical Assembly and the Jewish Theological Seminary or its duly authorized representatives, to decide what action by either spouse is then appropriate under Jewish matrimonial law; and if either spouse shall fail to honor the demand of the other or to carry out the decision of the *Beth Din* or its representatives, then the other spouse may invoke any and all remedies available in civil law and equity to enforce compliance with the *Beth Din's* decision and this solemn obligation." (See page 94 below, "Remarriage Customs.")

The Marriage Altar

A wedding may take place with bride and groom standing together before the rabbi, or bride and groom may stand on one side of a table, the rabbi on the other. When a table is used, it should be properly covered. Often candles and a bouquet of flowers are appropriately arranged, making the table special, an altar before which bride and groom stand. In recent times, artists have lent their talents to the making of a special table, an altar for marriage.

There is no valid reason for positioning bride and groom in one way or another. Custom has it, nevertheless, that the groom stands to the left of the bride. A reason given is that, in this position, the groom can more easily place a ring upon her left hand. Yet, in other disciplines, again without reason, the bride stands to the right of the officiant and the groom to his left.

The Breaking of the Glass

At the conclusion of the service, it is customary for the groom to stamp upon and break a glass. The breaking of the glass is not part of the service. It takes place when the service is over. Unlike ritual practice, it carries with it no reference or statement. The glass is simply broken.

There is much curiosity concerning the source and purpose of this practice. What should be considered by those planning for a wedding is not the history of the practice but its contemporary significance.

A wedding is a tense experience, not only for the bride and groom, but also for the celebrants. The words read for the bride and groom are also heard by the assembled as meaningful commentary upon their lives. The tension builds up during the service to its very end. Seated or standing, the assembled are locked into an anxious moment that is shattered with the breaking of the glass. The tension is suddenly released. A spirit of gaiety takes hold and the celebration is well begun.

When a glass is to be broken, it should be a thin glass wrapped in cloth so that the shards are contained and no damage is done.

ADDITIONAL CUSTOMS AND PRACTICES

Honoring the Groom
The groom attends and is recognized at a Sabbath synagogue service prior to his wedding. He is invited to recite the blessings for the reading of the Torah. Thereafter a special prayer *(Mi Sheberach)* is offered on behalf of both the bride and groom. The congregation may respond with the showering of both bride and groom with almonds and raisins, symbolizing their prayers for the couple's success (and fertility). In the Talmud there is a reference to a similar practice in which roasted ears of corn mixed with nuts are used.

Circling the Groom
When the bride reaches the canpoy, before taking her place at the side of her groom, she circles him seven times. Some have changed this practice, reducing the circles to three. The practice has been ascribed to the poetry of the Prophet Hosea (2:19-20): "I will betroth thee unto me forever; I will betroth thee unto me in righteousness, justice, loving kindness, mercy; I will betroth thee unto me in faithfulness."

Ritual Immersion—The *Mikveh*
The sanctity of the body is a serious concern in Orthodox Judaism. The tradition calls upon woman and man, with special emphasis upon woman, to cleanse themselves, ritually, in waters prepared and gathered into a *mikveh*. Within four days of a wedding, a bride immerses herself and is cleansed for her wedding.

Bride and Groom Refrain from Seeing Each Other
Bride and groom refrain from seeing each other on the day of the wedding until the time, or immediately before, the service when the groom and witnesses approach the bride and the veil is put in place.

The *Kittel*
The *kittel* is a white robe, reminiscent of a shroud, which among some traditionalists is worn during the prayer service on the Day of Atonement. It is also worn by a groom during his wedding service.

Wedding Day Fast
Bride and groom fast from sunrise on the day of their wedding until the wedding meal is served. Fasting does not take place on Sabbaths, holy days, or festivals. It is a symbol of sacrifice, giving up one's

needs to prove one's worth. It is also a symbol of atonement, a cleansing of the self of all sins prior to the marriage. For the devout, the confessional prayers recited on the Day of Atonement are read prior to the wedding.

Wedding Meal

In the planning of a wedding celebration, the practices of the guests should be taken into consideration, lest they be offended by the food served to them. If the guests are inclined toward the observance of the laws of *kashrut,* then certainly those planning for the wedding will want to plan for a kosher meal. If the meal is not kosher, but some guests do follow *kashrut,* special provisions should be made for them. A special meal could be delivered by a kosher caterer, as they do for airline passengers, or a special dish could be prepared for them (usually fish in the place of meat).

There is also a meal that is best described as "kosher style," in which forbidden foods are not served and the general practice of separating meats and dairy foods is maintained.

The Invocation

A wedding meal is special and should be made so, not only with the ceremony of the wedding cake at the end of the meal, but with an invocation at the beginning. The practice of having bride and groom cut the *chalah* (The Festival Bread) lends a note of sanctity to the meal. Two blessings may be recited prior to the meal.

> We give praise to You, Lord of our destinies, You who have kept us alive, sustained us and brought us together that we might rejoice in the blessing that is now upon us.
>
> We give praise to You, Lord of our world, Who brings forth the bounty of His blessings from the earth.

The *Yarmulka (Kipah)*

The *yarmulka,* or head covering, is a symbol of Jewish religious life and has taken on a quality other than that originally intended, namely, one of identification. The simple black *yarmulka* has given way to a variety of colors and embroidered designs. It is used at weddings, worn by the assembled males, or by the groom and his attendants. In keeping with a need or a desire to constantly dramatize the wedding experience, people have taken to printing the names of the bride and groom on the lining of the *yarmulka.*

Traditional Judaism requires a head covering for religious services. Liberal Judaism does not. A wedding, however, brings together guests of various religious persuasions. If there may be guests who want *yarmulkas* and would feel uncomfortable without them, they should be provided.

When Death Occurs

In Jewish tradition, there is a compelling need to respect the dead. When the death of a parent, grandparent, or sibling takes place preceding a wedding, the question arises as to whether or not the initial plans, if carried out, would dishonor the deceased. The answer to this question will vary from family to family, from situation to situation.

Depending upon the relationship of the mourner to the deceased, the full year of death is a period of mourning. During these periods the personal practices of the mourners are confined to the essentials of living. Sybaritic celebrations are forbidden, while those commanded by faith are not only permitted, but required. They are of the *mitzvot* of life, and a wedding is a *mitzvah*. Its celebration should not conflict with the primary periods of mourning.

If the wedding is planned for a time beyond *sheloshim* (the first thirty days after death) and if it is acceptable to those involved, the continuation of the plans should pose no problem. However, the celebration should be subdued as a mark of respect for the deceased. If the wedding was scheduled for the period of *sheloshim* and for good reason must take place in that period, a simple service without the usual noises and forms of celebration would be in order, as long as those in attendance understand and appreciate the circumstances that brought on the decision. If the deceased left word that the wedding was to proceed as planned, then the wedding takes place in accordance with the wishes of the deceased as a mark of respect for the person and the request.

When a parent has died, a Remembrance Prayer may be included as part of the wedding service. There is a question, however, as to the advisability of introducing so sad a note into the wedding festivity. For those who would want the Remembrance Prayer and at the same time to keep the spirit of the wedding as joyous as possible, an alternate practice is suggested. The family of the deceased, together with the bride and groom, gather before the wedding service in a special place where the rabbi reflects upon the practice of remembering the deceased, especially at a time when his/her child is about to be married. The rabbi concludes with the Remembrance Prayer, and then says: "And let us now proceed with the *mitzvah* of marriage."

93

REMARRIAGE CUSTOMS

We cannot escape the fact that divorce is very much a part of the rhythm of life. The rate of divorce has climbed precipitously, and today one of every two marriages will end in divorce.

Divorced people remarry. In Jewish practice, there is the tradition of the *Get*, the religious sanction of a divorce, without which a remarriage cannot take place.

To understand the *Get*, one must be aware of the nature of that Jewish community in which the responsibility for the marriage covenant was vested in the hands of religious authorities, who functioned according to a set code of laws ordained by a long and continuing tradition. The engagement and marriage were recorded, with all their particulars, in a set of legal documents. Likewise, a divorce had to comply with established procedure and be sanctioned by the authorities. The particulars of the divorce were contained in an instrument known as the *Get*.

A problem arises in our times among those complying with the tradition of the *Get*, in that the *Get* can only be given by the husband to the wife; the wife cannot divorce her husband. In the bitterness that often brings on a divorce, the husband may refuse to give his wife a *Get*, or he may extract concessions to which he might not be justly entitled. There is little the authorities can do when a husband refuses to grant a *Get*. He may remarry without difficulty, but his former wife remains in limbo until such time as a *Get* is produced. Those who strive to maintain this tradition have sought to develop a procedure that would be responsive to the needs of the wife. The Conservative rabbinate has addressed the problem by inserting in the marriage *Ketubah* a statement in which the bride and groom commit to a procedure which would attend the wife's needs in case of a divorce. (See pages 89-90 above, "The Text of the Conservative *Ketubah*.")

For Liberal (Reform) Judaism, marriage and divorce are the responsibility of the state, and there is no need for the "legal" *Ketubah* or *Get*. Liberal Jews maintain that a marriage or divorce sanctioned by the state cannot be questioned by any of the religious disciplines that make up the American society. Thus, the absence of a *Get* is not a hindrance to a remarriage among Liberal Jews.

MUSIC

The following musical compositions are available through music publishers and book stores dealing with Judaica.

Traditional Wedding Music
- Adler, *The Wedding Ceremony*
- Davidson, Helfman, Meisels, Secunda, & Weiner, *Music for the Jewish Wedding*
- Nulman, *Wedding Service*
- Barash, *Sheva Berachot*
- Isaacson, *Kol Sason*
- Kasakoff, *Music for the Jewish Wedding*
- Kopmar, *Wedding Service,* scored for flute/guitar
- Gold, *Wedding Service,* scored for organ, piano, string quartet
- Taube, Kuchinsky, *Wedding Service*
- Miron, *Sheva Berachot*
- Weiner, Y., *Wedding Service*
- Alter, *Sheva Berachot*

Individual Compositions
- Goldman, *Song of Ruth*
- Binder, *Ani Chavatzelet ha-Sharon*
- Alman, *Et Kol Libah*
- Steinberg, *Ve-Erastich Li*
- Sinsheimer, *I Will Betrothe You*
- Neumann, *Yom Gila*
- Rossi, *Baruch ha-Ba*
- Kingsley, *Rise up My Beloved*
- Hemsi, *Ah, The Groom*
- Algazzi, *Golden Ladder*
- Schiff, *Wedding Verses*
- Berman, *Set Me as a Seal*
- Vinever, *Wedding Nigun*
- Adler, *Set Me as a Seal*
- Binder, *Lord, Do Thou Consider*
- Barkan, *Hark, My Beloved*
- Janowsky, *Ana Dodi*
- Schalit, *Wedding Song*
- Helfman, *Ana Dodi*
- Saminsky, *Shir ha-Shirim*
- Kasakoff, *My Beloved and I*
- Idelsohn, *Set Me as a Seal*
- Reznick, *A Seal Upon Thy Heart*
- Miron, *Ha-Yafa ba-Nashim*
- Adler, *A Woman of Valor*
- Bugatch, *Ani Chavatzelet ha-Sharon*

95

Processionals and Recessionals
- Davidson, *Four Marches*
- Freed, *Postludium*
- Meyerbeer, *Coronation March*
- Berlinski, *Processional*
- Tedesco, *Processional*
- Weinberg, *Processional*
- Bloch, *Four Wedding Marches*
- Painter, *Two Festive Marches*
- Brenner, *Processional*
- Ellstein, *Processional*

REFORM WEDDING SERVICE

RABBI:

בָּרוּךְ הַבָּא בְּשֵׁם יְיָ, בֵּרַכְנוּכֶם מִבֵּית יְיָ.
אֵלִי אַתָּה וְאוֹדֶךָ, אֱלֹהַי אֲרוֹמְמֶךָ.
הוֹדוּ לַיְיָ כִּי טוֹב, כִּי לְעוֹלָם חַסְדּוֹ.
מִי אַדִּיר עַל הַכֹּל, מִי בָּרוּךְ עַל הַכֹּל, מִי גָּדוֹל עַל הַכֹּל, יְבָרֵךְ אֶת־הֶחָתָן
וְאֶת־הַכַּלָּה.

O God, supremely blessed, supreme in might and glory, guide and bless this groom and bride.

Standing here in the presence of God, the Guardian of the home, ready to enter into the bond of wedlock, answer in the fear of God, and in the hearing of those assembled:

Do you, _____, of your own free will and consent take _____ to be your wife/husband and do you promise to love, honor, and cherish her/him throughout life?

GROOM/BRIDE: I do.

The Benedictions
RABBI:

בָּרוּךְ אַתָּה, יְיָ אֱלֹהֵינוּ, מֶלֶךְ הָעוֹלָם, שֶׁהַכֹּל בָּרָא לִכְבוֹדוֹ.

We give praise to God, Master of the Universe in which all creation reflects upon His glory.

בָּרוּךְ אַתָּה, יְיָ אֱלֹהֵינוּ, מֶלֶךְ הָעוֹלָם, יוֹצֵר הָאָדָם.

We give praise to God, Master of the Universe—He Who has created you, His children.

בָּרוּךְ אַתָּה, יְיָ אֱלֹהֵינוּ, מֶלֶךְ הָעוֹלָם, אֲשֶׁר יָצַר אֶת־הָאָדָם בְּצַלְמוֹ, בְּצֶלֶם
דְּמוּת תַּבְנִיתוֹ, וְהִתְקִין לוֹ מִמֶּנּוּ בִּנְיַן עֲדֵי עַד. בָּרוּךְ אַתָּה, יְיָ, יוֹצֵר הָאָדָם.

96

We give praise to God, Master of the Universe—He Who created man and woman in His image. With them and through them, may His will for the Universe be manifest. Blessed is He, the Creator of His people.

בָּרוּךְ אַתָּה, יְיָ אֱלֹהֵינוּ, מֶלֶךְ הָעוֹלָם, אֲשֶׁר בָּרָא שָׂשׂוֹן וְשִׂמְחָה, חָתָן וְכַלָּה, גִּילָה רִנָּה דִּיצָה וְחֶדְוָה, אַהֲבָה וְאַחֲוָה, שָׁלוֹם וְרֵעוּת. שַׂמֵּחַ תְּשַׂמַּח רֵעִים הָאֲהוּבִים, וְיִזְכּוּ לִבְנוֹת בַּיִת בְּיִשְׂרָאֵל לְשֵׁם וְלִתְהִלָּה, וִיהִי שָׁלוֹם בְּבֵיתָם וְשַׁלְוָה וְהַשְׁקֵט בְּלִבּוֹתָם, וְיִרְאוּ בְנֶחָמַת יִשְׂרָאֵל וּבִתְשׁוּעַת עוֹלָם. בָּרוּךְ אַתָּה, יְיָ, מְשַׂמֵּחַ חָתָן עִם הַכַּלָּה.

The Wine Service

RABBI: Unto You, our Father, we lift our souls in praise. As all creation reflects Your glory, even so _____ and _____, fashioned in Your image, reveal Your majesty. Within their hearts did You implant the enobling impulses of love and devotion. Source of all life and all joy, sanctify the covenant which _____ and _____ are consummating in Your Name. Bestow upon them Your gifts of friendship, of love, and of peace. Make them rejoice in the sweetness of that family union which is founded on honesty and fidelity, on duty and religious consecration. Be with them at this hour of their gladness, bless their covenant and seal their bond of wedlock with love everlasting.

בָּרוּךְ אַתָּה, יְיָ אֱלֹהֵינוּ, מֶלֶךְ הָעוֹלָם, בּוֹרֵא פְּרִי הַגָּפֶן.

We give praise to You, Lord, Master of our destinies, Who has created the fruit of the vine.

Bride and Groom drink of the cup.

RABBI: As together you now drink from this cup, so may you, under God's guidance, in perfect union and devotion to each other, draw contentment, comfort and felicity from the cup of life, and thereby may you find life's joys doubly gladdening, its bitterness sweetened, and all things hallowed by true companionship and love.

The Ring Service

RABBI: And now, _____, place this ring upon the finger of your bride/groom as a token of wedlock and repeat these words:

Be thou consecrated unto me with this ring as my wife/husband, according to the laws of Moses and Israel.

הֲרֵי אַתְּ מְקֻדֶּשֶׁת לִי בְּטַבַּעַת זוֹ כְּדַת מֹשֶׁה וְיִשְׂרָאֵל.

Bride and Groom repeat.

RABBI: As by these rings you symbolize your marriage bond, may their meaning sink into your hearts and bind your lives together by

97

devotion and faithfulness one to another. In mutual self-consecration and in ever-deepening love for one another, may you
establish a beautiful and a meaningful home among us, a home
filled with spirit of faith, truth, and the fear of God. Praised be
You, O Lord, Who does sanctify these your children, _____
and _____, by the holy covenant of marriage.

בָּרוּךְ אַתָּה, יְיָ, מְקַדֵּשׁ עַמּוֹ יִשְׂרָאֵל עַל יְדֵי (חֻפָּה וְ) קִדּוּשִׁין.

Now that you have spoken the words and performed the rites
which unite your lives, I do hereby, in conformity with the faith
of Judaism, and the laws of this State, declare your marriage
valid and binding; and I pronounce you, _____ and
_____, to be husband and wife before God and peoples
everywhere.

The Benediction
RABBI:

יְבָרֶכְךָ יְיָ וְיִשְׁמְרֶךָ.
יָאֵר יְיָ פָּנָיו אֵלֶיךָ וִיחֻנֶּךָּ.
יִשָּׂא יְיָ פָּנָיו אֵלֶיךָ וְיָשֵׂם לְךָ שָׁלוֹם.

May the Lord bless you and keep you.
May the Lord let His countenance shine upon you and be
gracious to you.
May the Lord lift up His countenance upon you and give you
peace. AMEN.

A glass may be broken.

Notes on the Service

A homily or sermon may be included, lending a personal note to
the service. Its place in the service and the manner in which it is introduced reflect a rabbinical preference.

In this service only three of the seven marriage blessings are included. The theme of the remaining blessings is expressed in the
paragraph following the blessings. At the request of the bride and
groom, the full seven blessings may be included in the service.

ORTHODOX WEDDING SERVICE

The text of the Orthodox service is in Hebrew. In the reading of the
service, a rabbi may translate portions or insert special English readings.

RABBI:

מִי אַדִּיר עַל הַכֹּל,
מִי בָּרוּךְ עַל הַכֹּל,

98

מִי גָדוֹל עַל הַכֹּל,
יְבָרֵךְ חָתָן וְכַלָּה.

He Who is supremely mighty,
He Who is supremely praised,
He Who is supremely great—
May He bless this groom and bride.

As the Bride is escorted to the canopy, the following is said.

RABBI:

אַדִּיר אֱלֹהֵינוּ.
סִימָן טוֹב וּמַזָּל טוֹב.
חָתָן בָּרוּךְ הוּא.
כַּלָּה בְּרוּכָה וְנָאָה.

Mighty is our God.
Auspicious signs and good fortune.
Praiseworthy is the bridegroom.
Praiseworthy and handsome is the bride.

The Bride circles the Groom seven or three times, as the custom may be.

The Wedding Address

Betrothal Benedictions

RABBI:

בָּרוּךְ אַתָּה, יְיָ אֱלֹהֵינוּ, מֶלֶךְ הָעוֹלָם, בּוֹרֵא פְּרִי הַגָּפֶן.
בָּרוּךְ אַתָּה, יְיָ אֱלֹהֵינוּ, מֶלֶךְ הָעוֹלָם, אֲשֶׁר קִדְּשָׁנוּ בְּמִצְוֹתָיו וְצִוָּנוּ עַל
הָעֲרָיוֹת, וְאָסַר לָנוּ אֶת־הָאֲרוּסוֹת, וְהִתִּיר לָנוּ אֶת־הַנְּשׂוּאוֹת לָנוּ עַל
יְדֵי חֻפָּה וְקִדּוּשִׁין. בָּרוּךְ אַתָּה, יְיָ, מְקַדֵּשׁ עַמּוֹ יִשְׂרָאֵל עַל יְדֵי חֻפָּה
וְקִדּוּשִׁין.

Praised be Thou, O Lord our God, King of the Universe, Who
has created the fruit of the vine.

Praised be Thou, O Lord our God, King of the Universe, Who
has sanctified us with His commandments, and has commanded us concerning forbidden connections, and has forbidden us
those who are merely betrothed, but has allowed us those lawfully married to us through *Chuppah* and betrothal. Praised be
Thou, O Lord, Who sanctifies Thy people Israel through *Chuppah* and betrothal.

*Bride and Groom partake of a cup of wine. Groom places a ring on the finger of
his bride and recites:*

GROOM:

הֲרֵי אַתְּ מְקֻדֶּשֶׁת לִי בְּטַבַּעַת זוֹ כְּדַת מֹשֶׁה וְיִשְׂרָאֵל.

Be thou consecrated to me with this ring in accordance
with the laws of Moses and Israel.

The Ketubah *is read. A second full cup of wine is held by the rabbi as he recites:*

RABBI:

בָּרוּךְ אַתָּה, יְיָ אֱלֹהֵינוּ, מֶלֶךְ הָעוֹלָם, בּוֹרֵא פְּרִי הַגָּפֶן.
בָּרוּךְ אַתָּה, יְיָ אֱלֹהֵינוּ, מֶלֶךְ הָעוֹלָם, שֶׁהַכֹּל בָּרָא לִכְבוֹדוֹ.

בָּרוּךְ אַתָּה, יְיָ אֱלֹהֵינוּ, מֶלֶךְ הָעוֹלָם, יוֹצֵר הָאָדָם.

בָּרוּךְ אַתָּה, יְיָ אֱלֹהֵינוּ, מֶלֶךְ הָעוֹלָם, אֲשֶׁר יָצַר אֶת־הָאָדָם בְּצַלְמוֹ, בְּצֶלֶם דְּמוּת תַּבְנִיתוֹ, וְהִתְקִין לוֹ מִמֶּנּוּ בִּנְיַן עֲדֵי עַד. בָּרוּךְ אַתָּה, יְיָ, יוֹצֵר הָאָדָם.

שׂוֹשׂ תָּשִׂישׂ וְתָגֵל הָעֲקָרָה בְּקִבּוּץ בָּנֶיהָ לְתוֹכָהּ בְּשִׂמְחָה. בָּרוּךְ אַתָּה, יְיָ, מְשַׂמֵּחַ צִיּוֹן בְּבָנֶיהָ.

שַׂמֵּחַ תְּשַׂמַּח רֵעִים הָאֲהוּבִים, כְּשַׂמֵּחֲךָ יְצִירְךָ בְּגַן עֵדֶן מִקֶּדֶם. בָּרוּךְ אַתָּה, יְיָ, מְשַׂמֵּחַ חָתָן וְכַלָּה.

בָּרוּךְ אַתָּה, יְיָ אֱלֹהֵינוּ, מֶלֶךְ הָעוֹלָם, אֲשֶׁר בָּרָא שָׂשׂוֹן וְשִׂמְחָה, חָתָן וְכַלָּה, גִּילָה רִנָּה דִּיצָה וְחֶדְוָה, אַהֲבָה וְאַחֲוָה, שָׁלוֹם וְרֵעוּת. מְהֵרָה, יְיָ אֱלֹהֵינוּ, יִשָּׁמַע בְּעָרֵי יְהוּדָה וּבְחוּצוֹת יְרוּשָׁלַיִם קוֹל שָׂשׂוֹן וְקוֹל שִׂמְחָה, קוֹל חָתָן וְקוֹל כַּלָּה, קוֹל מִצְהֲלוֹת חֲתָנִים מֵחֻפָּתָם וּנְעָרִים מִמִּשְׁתֵּה נְגִינָתָם. בָּרוּךְ אַתָּה, יְיָ, מְשַׂמֵּחַ חָתָן עִם הַכַּלָּה.

Praised are You, O Lord our God, King of the Universe, Creator of the fruit of the vine.

Praised are You, O Lord our God, King of the Universe, Who created all things for Your glory.

Praised are You, O Lord our God, King of the Universe, Creator of man.

Praised are You, O Lord our God, King of the Universe, Who created man and woman in His image, fashioning woman from man as his mate, that together they might perpetuate life. Praised are You, O Lord, Creator of man.

May Zion rejoice as her children are restored to her in joy. Praised are You, O Lord, Who grants the joy of bride and groom.

Grant perfect joy to these loving companions, as You did to the first man and woman in the Garden of Eden. Praised are You, O Lord, Who grants the joy of bride and groom.

Praised are You, O Lord our God, King of the Universe, Who created joy and gladness, bride and groom, mirth, song, delight and rejoicing, love and harmony, peace and companionship. O Lord our God, may there ever be heard in the cities of Judah and in the streets of Jerusalem voices of joy and gladness, voices of bride and groom, the jubilant voices of those joined in marriage under the bridal canopy, the voices of young people feasting and singing. Praised are You, O Lord, Who causes the groom to rejoice with his bride.

The cup of wine is presented to the Bridegroom and to the Bride.

CONSERVATIVE WEDDING SERVICE

Processional

Betrothal Service
All members of the bridal party take their places under the Chuppah.

RABBI: בָּרוּךְ הַבָּא בְּשֵׁם יְיָ.

May you who are here be blessed in the name of the Lord.

If the ceremony takes place in a synagogue:

RABBI: בֵּרַכְנוּכֶם מִבֵּית יְיָ.

We bless you from the house of the Lord.

מִי אַדִּיר עַל הַכֹּל, מִי בָּרוּךְ עַל הַכֹּל, מִי גָּדוֹל עַל הַכֹּל, הוּא יְבָרֵךְ הֶחָתָן וְהַכַּלָּה.

May He Who is supreme in power, blessing, and glory bless this bridegroom and this bride.

The rabbi may offer a prayer as follows:

RABBI: Our heavenly Father, Source of holiness, help us to see the sacred dimension of all life. Guide this bridegroom and this bride to the realization of sanctity and devotion every day as to-day. Help them to renew their love continually, as You renew Creation. May their concern for each other reflect Your concern for all men; may their loving faithfulness reflect Your love. Throughout the years may they hallow their life together, that the home they establish become a blessing to all Israel. May Your light illumine their lives. And let us say: AMEN.

The first cup of wine is lifted.

RABBI: בָּרוּךְ אַתָּה, יְיָ אֱלֹהֵינוּ, מֶלֶךְ הָעוֹלָם, בּוֹרֵא פְּרִי הַגָּפֶן.
בָּרוּךְ אַתָּה, יְיָ אֱלֹהֵינוּ, מֶלֶךְ הָעוֹלָם, אֲשֶׁר קִדְּשָׁנוּ בְּמִצְוֹתָיו וְצִוָּנוּ עַל הָעֲרָיוֹת, וְאָסַר לָנוּ אֶת הָאֲרוּסוֹת, וְהִתִּיר לָנוּ אֶת הַנְּשׂוּאוֹת לָנוּ עַל יְדֵי חֻפָּה וְקִדּוּשִׁין. בָּרוּךְ אַתָּה, יְיָ, מְקַדֵּשׁ עַמּוֹ יִשְׂרָאֵל עַל יְדֵי חֻפָּה וְקִדּוּשִׁין.

Groom and Bride partake of the wine.

RABBI: As you share the wine of this cup, so may you share all things from this day on with love and with understanding.

The Marriage Service
The ring is placed by the Groom upon the right forefinger of his bride.

GROOM: הֲרֵי אַתְּ מְקֻדֶּשֶׁת לִי בְּטַבַּעַת זוּ כְּדַת מֹשֶׁה וְיִשְׂרָאֵל.

101

By this ring you are consecrated to me as my wife in accordance with with law of Moses and the people Israel.

The Ketubah *is read. The Conservative service does not include an exchange of rings; if a double ring service is required, following the reading of the* Ketubah, *the Bride may place a ring of the finger of her groom and say:*

BRIDE: This ring is a symbol that you are my husband, and a sign of my love and devotion.

A homily or sermon may be offered, concluding with:

RABBI: Since both of you have joined voluntarily in this ceremony which binds you together in marriage, abiding by the laws of the State (Commonwealth) (Province) of _____ and acting in accordance with the law of Moses and the people Israel, you, _____, and you, _____, are now husband and wife.

Benediction

RABBI:

יְבָרֶכְךָ יְיָ וְיִשְׁמְרֶךָ.

יָאֵר יְיָ פָּנָיו אֵלֶיךָ וִיחֻנֶּךָ.

יִשָּׂא יְיָ פָּנָיו אֵלֶיךָ וְיָשֵׂם לְךָ שָׁלוֹם.

May the Lord bless you, and guard you.
May the Lord show you favor, and be gracious to you.
May the Lord show you kindness and grant you peace. AMEN.

The Groom breaks a glass.

Notes on the Service

Orthodox and Conservative practices combine an engagement *(Erusin)* and marriage *(Nisu'in)* declaration in a single service. A cup of wine is used for each service.

During periods in history when Jewish law prevailed and when families arranged or contracted for the marriage of children, the particulars of an arrangement (engagement) were recorded in a documents known as an *Agreement (Tena'im)*. Once this agreement was confirmed, the couple were bound to each other, though they did not live together. The agreement could not be broken without juridical consent (a divorce). The wedding followed, with the *Ketubah*, including the particulars of the agreement that had been negotiated. With the radical change from the arranged to the romantic marriage, the engagement agreement no longer commanded the interests and concerns of the people. But, as is the way of tradition, the remembrance of that practice is represented in the *Erusin* service that takes place immediately before the *Nisu'in*, the marriage service.

102

A RESPONSIVE MARRIAGE SERVICE

Processional

Words of Welcome
FAMILY
REPRESENTATIVE: Assembled friends, witnesses to the miracle of love, out of affection for _____ and _____, we have gathered together to touch them with our hearts and our hopes as they speak their love for and commitment to each other.

To this moment they bring the fullness of their hearts, a treasure to be shared. They bring dreams that pierce their souls, a personality and a spirit, uniquely their own, and out of which, we pray, will grow the reality of their togetherness.

We rejoice with them, the outward symbol of an inward union of hearts emerging out of friendship, respect and love.

We greet you on behalf of _____ and _____, their parents and families, and call upon you to support them in their sacred resolve and to share this and all the joys God will bestow upon them.

Prayer
BRIDE: I will greatly rejoice in the Lord,
My soul shall be joyful in my God;
For He hath clothed me in the garments of salvation.
He hath covered me with the role of victory
As a bridegroom putteth on a priestly crown
And a bride adorneth herself with her jewels.

GROOM: And I will look at you
And see beyond the shadows;
You will look at me
And see beyond the form to my substance.
Together we will see glorious things
No one has seen before.
We will see them in each other
And make them so.

BRIDE: We will forget
All who knew us falsely,

103

> Partially,
> Who did not know us at all.
> We will lift our eyes from the detail,
> Turn from the habit
> Of approving and disapproving.
> We will lift our eyes to the vision,
> See the good and the bad,
> The happy and the sorrowful,
> And accept it all with joy.
> And thus we say,
> For the first time in our lives,
> I—Thou.

GROOM: For as the earth bringeth forth her growth,
And as the garden causeth things sown to spring forth,
So the Lord will cause victory and glory
To spring forth before all nations.

The Blessings

The traditional seven blessings (Sheva Berachot) *are said here (see previous services).*

GROOM: How will I know you?
I will know you by your song,
And I will know you by your smile.
I will look at you and see a strength
I have never seen before.
And I will behold a sensitivity in you,
Companion to your strength.
I will find myself encircled by your glow,
And in it we will walk, together, always.

BRIDE: How will I know you?
I cannot know
What words you will speak,
But when you say them,
I will know you.
And as you listen
For the things I say
And the words I leave unspoken,
So will you also know me.
My words, joined with yours,
Will drench the earth around us.

The Vows

RABBI: Do you, _____, of your own free will and consent, take
_____ to be your wife/husband; and do you promise to love,
honor and cherish her/him throughout your life?

104

GROOM/BRIDE: Yes, I, _____, choose you, _____, to be my wife/
husband—my friend, my love, the mother/father of
our children. I will be yours in plenty and in want, in
sickness and in health, in failure and in triumph. I will
cherish you and respect you, comfort and encourage
you, and together we shall live, freed and bound by
our love.

ATTENDANT ONE: Lord, thank You for the gift of love,
The love that brings us together.
Thank You for the gift of marriage
In which two people become more than they
   are.
Thank You for the privilege of witnessing
The commitment made by _____
   and _____
To each other in marriage.

ATTENDANT TWO: Lord, I feel You want love to grow.
Help, I pray You, the love of _____
   and _____.
As beautiful as it is, let it grow,
Grow deeply, entwining one another.
Lord, I feel You have made us
More beautiful than we know.
Help, I pray You, _____ and _____
To discern the beauty in each other
And within themselves
As they weave their years together.

ATTENDANT THREE: I believe there is conflict in every relation,
And I pray, Lord, help them
Deal openly and creatively with conflict,
Not only by speaking, but by listening.
May they learn to make allowances
Toward the fulfillment of their wish
One for another.

ATTENDANT FOUR: Lord, I pray, from them we might learn
More about love, and the power of love,
To create, to heal, and to build
Your city upon earth.

The Ring Service

RABBI: And now to symbolize your marriage, take this ring and place it
upon _____'s finger and as you do so, repeat these words:

הֲרֵי אַתְּ מְקֻדֶּשֶׁת לִי בְּטַבַּעַת זוּ כְּדַת מֹשֶׁה וְיִשְׂרָאֵל.

Be thou consecrated to me as my wife/husband in accordance with the tradition of Moses and Israel.

Weddings

The Groom and Bride repeat these words.

The Pronouncement

The Benediction

The Breaking of a Glass

Interfaith
Weddings

Interfaith marriages have become common in American society. Contemporary social, economic, and cultural conditions have contributed to this development. People of different faiths, contemplating marriage, may or may not have difficulties when making plans for an interfaith wedding.

A mixed marriage engenders deep feelings among people generally and evokes expressions of strong convictions among religious leaders. Families are known to reject a child who comes bearing news that he or she has chosen to marry "out of the faith." Clergypersons, likewise, have issued forth religious injunctions in the hope of discouraging mixed marriages.

Aside from institutional responses to mixed marriages, cultures generally resist interfaith marriages because they represent an incursion upon established expectations. A child embodies and represents a family's value system. When the child brings home a stranger, "one who is not like us," there is the fear the child will be lost to the family and the continuity of all it represents.

Furthermore, through a child, a family is extended. All families want to feel comfortable with the "new" family member a child brings into the community by way of marriage. Thus, families who fear that a new family member will, by his or her "strangeness," inhibit a free emotional sharing in their customs and practices are likely to resist the decision.

The Bible, a significant commentary on human aspiration, draws the reader into the mixed marriage experience with the story of the patriarch Abraham and his concern for his son Isaac. Abraham speaks to the master of his household and extracts from him a promise that, when the time comes for his son to marry, he will be restrained from taking a wife from among the women of the surrounding tribes. Instead, he, the aide, is to travel to Abraham's ancestral home and there, in the tribal family, search out a proper wife for Isaac.

Abraham left his family years before in search of a way of life different from that of his clanspeople. Now that he is well established in a new place and a new faith, he is still intent upon keeping the marriage of his son within the extended family.

The aide responds to Abraham: "I will go as you bid me. Supposing, in my going and my making a choice, the woman refuses to come with me back to this, your home. Shall I then take Isaac to Haran?"

The reader can feel the intensity with which Abraham cautions his aide when he responds: "Under no circumstances are you to return my son to Haran. If the woman refuses, you are then free of the promise you have made to me."

Abraham was caught up in a conflict of desires. He wanted his son to marry within the family. At the same time he wanted him to inherit and represent the cultural ways he had innovated. If he could have both, well and good. If not, he would take the cultural vision he hoped his son would represent, and allow him a marriage with a woman of a neighboring tribe.

The Abrahamitic conflict of family and culture is inescapable in American society, structured as it is on the compelling spirit of democracy. Marriages will in increasing numbers continue to override the injunctions of faith. When people contemplate such marriages, they would do well to understand that overcoming the injunctions does not negate the forces that have conditioned their being. Marriage does not change a person, nor does "love conquer all." These forces will manifest themselves in unanticipated ways in the course of marriage. It is important, therefore, for couples contemplating a mixed marriage to avail themselves of counseling that will help them understand the nature of their decision and marriage.

THE SERVICE

The interfaith service may be read by a clergyperson representing the faith of bride or groom. It may also be ecumenical in that both bride and groom are represented by their clergypersons.

THE CHILD OF A MIXED MARRIAGE

A question invariably discussed at premarital sessions focuses upon the rearing of a child in a mixed marriage. Bride and groom usually imply, in their analysis of their commitment to each other, that they are able to cope with the differences in their respective faiths and families. But how are children to be cared for and how will they respond to their mixed heritage?

First, they may consider preserving their respective faiths and sharing them with their children. In situations where the faiths are not radically different, a child can be made to feel comfortable with both traditions. It should be known, however, that though we speak of faiths as religious disciplines, they are also socially defined and our associations with them are often socially compelled. In sharing these traditions, comparable as they may be, one of them may be "better" than the other in that the child associates it with the preferred parent. When the faiths are radically different in theology and symbol, a sharing of faiths poses problems which the child may be unable to handle. The child may internalize the problems and be unable to identify with the faith of either parent.

A second approach is to discount the differences and emphasize what are believed to be the common goals of religious experience, namely, to "do justly, love mercy, and walk humbly with God." This is an oversimplification of the religious experience. There is a dream sequence in the biblical book of Genesis that annotates the religious experience. In his dream, young Jacob sees a ladder standing on the ground, its upper rungs reaching into the heavens. Upon this ladder he sees angels going up and returning, symbolizing an urge to tie together heaven and earth, the known and the unknown, penetrating the mystery of life itself. The reduction of these compelling needs to a series of ethical verities represents a misunderstanding of the nature of the religious experience, which the child senses.

A third approach is to opt for one of the two faiths. Often, in the planning for a mixed marriage, the choice is made part of the "agreement" for marriage. The effectiveness of such a decision will depend upon the manner in which parents by "precept and example" convey their decision to the child.

Finally, there is the approach that says: We will rear our child in a free atmosphere, affording him or her opportunities to come to know the nature and substance of faiths generally, and then, when ready, the child will make a choice. This approach, seemingly reasonable, misunderstands the learning process. Learning is not a gathering of knowledge stored for a time when a decision is to be made. Decisions, emotionally charged, are made from moment to moment in the learning process. A child does not wait, but identifies with image and role from the very moment of awareness. To project a special time for decision is a wishful way of anticipating and resolving a problem.

Serious thought must be given to these issues since the child, upon arrival, will affect whatever prenuptial commitments parents may have made to each other.

PROTESTANT ATTITUDE TOWARD INTERFAITH MARRIAGE

Since the representations of Protestantism are many, attitudes toward and procedures regarding mixed marriages vary.

The guidelines for the wedding service published by the United Methodist Church include the statement:

> When couples come from different religious traditions, the minister should advise them on ecumenical courtesies and possibilities. If a Roman Catholic priest will share in the service, he should be invited to take part in the premarital discussions and plans. In the service itself, the ministers should share equally in the ritual.

ROMAN CATHOLIC ATTITUDE TOWARD INTERFAITH MARRIAGE

The Roman Catholic attitude is stated in a decree issued by Pope Paul VI and entitled "Apostolic Letter Determining Norms for Mixed Marriages." The decree left many decisions to the religious hierarchy of each country. In the United States, the National Conference of Catholic Bishops issued a document applying the Pope's guidelines:

> The priest will welcome a request for a mixed marriage and extend himself and his office in giving assistance to the prospective bride and groom in preparing for their marriage. In the assistance he gives in preparation for marriage between a Catholic and a non-Catholic, and in his continued efforts to help all married couples and families, the priest will endeavor to be in contact and

110

to co-operate with the minister or religious counsellor of the non-Catholic.

The guideline also considers the matter of children born in a mixed marriage and requires the Catholic to make, in writing or orally, the following promise:

> I reaffirm my faith in Jesus Christ and, with God's help, intend to continue living that faith in the Catholic Church. I promise to do all in my power to share the faith I have received with my children by having them baptized and reared as Catholics.

The non-Catholic is not asked to sign any papers or make any promises with regard to the rearing of children. The Church recommends that the non-Catholic be made aware of and understand the spouse's obligation as a Catholic.

In an ecumenical marriage between a Catholic and a non-Catholic, if the wedding takes place in the sanctuary of the religion of the non-Catholic, the priest requests a dispensation from his hierarchy. When given, it spells out what he may or may not do in the reading of the service. Generally, the dispensation will say that there is but a single officiant at a service. Therefore, he, the second participant, is limited to such matters as the reading of Scripture and the offering of prayer and benediction.

JEWISH ATTITUDE
TOWARD INTERFAITH MARRIAGE

Each of Judaism's three major groups—Orthodox, Conservative, and Reform—has a position on interfaith marriage. Orthodox and Conservative clergy refuse to officiate at a mixed marriage and fault those who enter into such a marriage. They rely on two principles for this position. The first is *Halachah,* canon law, as they interpret its evolution through Jewish history. For them, the offering of *Kiddushin,* marriage solemnization, is restricted to those who follow the "laws of Moses and Israel" (i.e., Jews). Secondly, they believe that a mixed marriage is a threat to the vitality and the future of Judaism. To officiate at such a service is to encourage its dilution.

Reform rabbis are divided on the matter. The Central Conference of American Rabbis has by resolution asked its constituents to refrain from officiating at mixed marriages. A substantial number of Reform rabbis do not abide by this resolution and do, under varying circumstances, officiate at interfaith marriages. However, not all of these will share in an ecumenical service.

Born of a Jewish Mother

Jewish canonical law states that a child born of a Jewish mother is Jewish. Thus, in the marriage of a Jewish woman and a non-Jewish man, no matter the nature of that marriage, if the woman has not converted, the offspring of the marriage are Jewish. Conversely, if the mother is not Jewish, even if her offspring are reared in the Jewish faith, they are not considered Jewish unless they formally convert.

This canonical position has stirred the convictions of religious leaders, especially those of the Reform community, who have called for its revision. The faith of a child, they reason, should be determined first by the intent of the family in the rearing of the child and second by the wishes of the child. Accordingly, the Central Conference of American Rabbis, in formal session, proposed and confirmed the patrilineal principle, which in effect gives to the father the same rights as those traditionally given the mother.

ORTHODOX CHRISTIAN ATTITUDE TOWARD INTERFAITH MARRIAGE

Mixed marriage is forbidden to Orthodox Christians by canon law (specifically canon 72 of the Sixth Ecumenical Council). Therefore, it is incumbent upon the priest to discourage the Orthodox person from entering into a marriage with one who is non-Orthodox. However, in accordance with the principle of *oikonomia,* which permits the Church to abstain from a strict application of canon law, consideration is given to an Orthodox Christian who wishes to marry a non-Orthodox.

The wedding must take place in the Orthodox tradition. The sacrament of marriage is not offered in the case of an Orthodox Christian and a nonbaptized individual. The participation of a non-Orthodox clergyman in the service is forbidden. At best he may be present, and at the conclusion of the service offer a word in benediction.

THE WEDDING SERVICE

If the wedding service is to be read by the minister of the bride or groom, he or she will plan the service in consultation with them. Generally it will reflect the minister's tradition. If it is to be an ecumenical service with the clergypersons of both bride and groom present, then the bride and groom will be asked to designate which of the clergy is to be in charge of the service. When the question is posed, couples are often reluctant to designate one above the other and wish that somehow the two could equally share in the service. Designating one as the clergy in charge does not argue against an equal sharing in the service. It merely indicates the procedure that is to be followed, and which clergyperson assumes the reponsibility for the planning of the wedding. When the wedding takes place in a sanctuary, it normally follows that the clergyperson of that sanctuary assumes the role of "clergyperson in charge." It is only when the wedding takes place outside of a sanctuary that the question is posed.

For a service to be truly ecumenical, it must be open to development. If either minister submits a condition, saying, "This must happen," "This must be said," or "This cannot happen or be said," then the service is not ecumenical. There are a number of ways in which an ecumenical service can be designed. One is for the bride and groom to prepare the text of the service. In this volume and elsewhere, there are sample services and texts, parts of which may respond to the wishes of bride and groom and may be ordered into a service. With an understanding of the purpose of the wedding ceremony, the prospective bride and groom can create a service that expresses their intent and promise.

Once the text is formulated, it is presented to the officiating clergy for their advice and consent. The bride and groom can then assign readings to each of the participants.

The service may also be designed by the participating clergy. Each selects parts of his or her service and together they fit them into a unified and effective experience. This is not a difficult effort. Since there are two dramatic moments in the wedding service—the recitation of the vows and the giving of rings—the planning of the service can begin with the selection of one of these moments by one clergyperson, and the second by the other. If one of the clergypersons is well known to one of the families, having shared much with them as their minister, then it would contribute to the warmth of the service if that clergyperson delivers the homily or sermon. The remaining parts of the service can easily be divided. The drama of the service and its ecumenical spirit are heightened when the various parts are intertwined, one voice and then the other weaving in and out of the service. Caution should be taken against repetitions in order to satisfy oneself that the service is equally divided. This, in effect, destroys the rhythm of the service.

CHANGES IN WEDDING SERVICES

Two kinds of changes in wedding services are usually requested. One pertains to the content and drama, the other to symbol and theology of the service.

Suggested changes in content and drama pose few problems. There may be objection to a particular innovation if it burdens or belittles the sanctity of the service. Generally, however, a literary or poetic reading; a personal set of vows; a wine or a candle-lighting service; a sharing of bread/wine, or the distribution of flowers—all are welcome additions to the service.

Textual changes which alter the theology of the service pose a more difficult problem. In a Jewish/Christian wedding, the Jewish partner may ask that there be no reference to the trinity. Conversely, the Christian may ask that the words "in accordance with the laws of Moses and Israel" be eliminated. Or bride and groom may take offense at the injunction that the marriage must remain valid "as long as you shall live," and request that the words be modified to read "as long as you shall love." A request for these and other changes cannot always be granted since they may contravene the theology of a given religious discipline. The bride and groom must understand that inviting a clergyperson to conduct or share in their wedding service does not give them the right to command changes in the clergy's religious visions and commitments.

TWO SERVICES

To satisfy their respective faiths, bride and groom may choose to have two wedding services, one in each of their religious disciplines. There is no reason why two services cannot be conducted, if there is good reason for each and if the drama can be retained. In various European countries a civil service is required before the religious service. Also, when bride and groom are married in one part of the country and wish, in the interest of family and friends, to bring them into the warmth of their decision, they may plan for a repeat service in another part of the country. However, when two services follow one another on the same day or within some days merely for the sake of appeasing one set of parents or another, the wedding services (especially the second of the two) lose excitement and drama. One of the services is known and understood to be perfunctory, an appeasement and not a wedding service.

114

When two services are planned, two licenses must be obtained. A certificate issued by the minister of the first is not a valid document for the minister of the second service. When applying for a license, a request should be made for two copies. One will be marked "For Religious Service."

CONVERSION FOR MARRIAGE

All religions welcome converts, but they do not encourage conversion for marriage. Religious leaders want their converts to come to the fold when compelled by a desire to believe and worship in accordance with their religious teachings. However, there is also a feeling that conversion encouraged by love and a desire to establish a harmonious home should be supported. Therefore, programs for conversion are generally offered by all religious disciplines. Procedures for conversion vary from religion to religion.

OBJECTIONS TO A MARRIAGE

Whatever objection one religious discipline or another may take to the solemnization of a marriage, once the state has issued a license and a wedding has taken place, that marriage is valid and of unquestionable legitimacy.

A JEWISH-CHRISTIAN INTERFAITH SERVICE

The Call to the Service
OFFICIANT:

בָּרוּךְ הַבָּא בְּשֵׁם יְיָ, בֵּרַכְנוּכֶם מִבֵּית יְיָ.
אֵלִי אַתָּה וְאוֹדֶךָ, אֱלֹהַי אֲרוֹמְמֶךָ.
הוֹדוּ לַיְיָ כִּי טוֹב, כִּי לְעוֹלָם חַסְדּוֹ.
מִי אַדִּיר עַל הַכֹּל, מִי בָרוּךְ עַל הַכֹּל, מִי גָּדוֹל עַל הַכֹּל, יְבָרֵךְ
אֶת־הֶחָתָן וְאֶת־הַכַּלָּה.

O, God, supremely blessed, supreme in might and glory, guide and bless this groom and bride.

Words of Welcome

Scriptural or Other Readings

115

Intent and Vows

*Intent and vows may take one of many forms. The Intent does not occur in all
services. It is an inquiry made of the Bride and Groom as to their intentions, and
may take the following form.*

OFFICIANT: Will you have this woman/man to be your wife/husband,
and will you promise, in all love and honor, in all duty and
service, in all faith and tenderness, to live with her/him,
and cherish her/him, according to the ordinance of God,
in the holy bond of marriage?

*The Intent is followed by a set of vows read by the officiant and repeated by the
Bride and Groom. It may take the following form.*

GROOM/BRIDE: I, _____, take you, _____, to be my wedded wife/
husband; and I promise and covenant, before God and
these witnesses, to be your loving and faithful hus-
band/wife, in plenty and in want, in joy and in sorrow,
in sickness and in health, as long as we shall both live.

*A simpler version is to omit the Intent and have the Bride and Groom respond to
a statement read by the officiant with the words, "I do." A text for the simpler version follows.*

OFFICIANT: Do you, _____, take _____ to be your lawfully wedded wife/husband, and do you promise to love, honor,
and cherish her/him as long you shall live/love?

The Marriage Blessings and Wine Service

OFFICIANT:

בָּרוּךְ אַתָּה, יְיָ אֱלֹהֵינוּ, מֶלֶךְ הָעוֹלָם, שֶׁהַכֹּל בָּרָא לִכְבוֹדוֹ.
בָּרוּךְ אַתָּה, יְיָ אֱלֹהֵינוּ, מֶלֶךְ הָעוֹלָם, יוֹצֵר הָאָדָם.
בָּרוּךְ אַתָּה, יְיָ אֱלֹהֵינוּ, מֶלֶךְ הָעוֹלָם, אֲשֶׁר יָצַר אֶת־הָאָדָם
בְּצַלְמוֹ, בְּצֶלֶם דְּמוּת תַּבְנִיתוֹ, וְהִתְקִין לוֹ מִמֶּנּוּ בִּנְיַן עֲדֵי עַד.
בָּרוּךְ אַתָּה, יְיָ, יוֹצֵר הָאָדָם.

בָּרוּךְ אַתָּה, יְיָ אֱלֹהֵינוּ, מֶלֶךְ הָעוֹלָם, אֲשֶׁר בָּרָא שָׂשׂוֹן וְשִׂמְחָה,
חָתָן וְכַלָּה, גִּילָה רִנָּה דִּיצָה וְחֶדְוָה, אַהֲבָה וְאַחֲוָה, שָׁלוֹם
וְרֵעוּת. שַׂמֵּחַ תְּשַׂמַּח רֵעִים הָאֲהוּבִים, וְיִזְכּוּ לִבְנוֹת בַּיִת
בְּיִשְׂרָאֵל לְשֵׁם וְלִתְהִלָּה, וִיהִי שָׁלוֹם בְּבֵיתָם וְשַׁלְוָה וְהַשְׁקֵט
בְּלִבּוֹתָם, וְיִרְאוּ בְּנֶחָמַת יִשְׂרָאֵל וּבִתְשׁוּעַת עוֹלָם. בָּרוּךְ אַתָּה,
יְיָ, מְשַׂמֵּחַ חָתָן עִם הַכַּלָּה.

Unto Thee, O God and Father, we lift our souls in
praise. As all creation reflects Thy glory, even so _____
and _____, fashioned in Thine image, reveal Thy majesty. Within their hearts didst Thou implant the enobling
impulses of love and devotion. Thou, Source of all life
and of all joy, sanctify the covenant which _____ and
_____ are consummating in Thy name. Bestow upon

116

them Thy gifts of friendship, of love, and of peace. Make them rejoice in the sweetness of that family union which is founded on purity and fidelity, on duty and religious consecration. Be with them at this hour of their gladness, bless their covenant, and seal their bond of wedlock with love everlasting. AMEN.

בָּרוּךְ אַתָּה, יְיָ אֱלֹהֵינוּ, מֶלֶךְ הָעוֹלָם, בּוֹרֵא פְּרִי הַגָּפֶן.

Praised be Thou, O God, King of the Universe, Who hast created the fruit of the vine.

Groom offers cup to Bride, and then drinks of it.

OFFICIANT: As together you now drink from this cup, so may you, under God's guidance, in perfect union and devotion to each other, draw contentment, comfort, and felicity from the cup of life, and thereby may you find life's joys doubly gladdening, its bitterness sweetened, and all things hallowed by true companionship and love.

The Ring Service

OFFICIANT *(to the Groom):*   And now, _____, place this ring upon the finger of your bride as token of wedlock, and repeat the words which I now say:

Be thou consecrated unto me with this ring as my wife, according to the faith of God and humanity.

The groom repeats the vow.

OFFICIANT *(to the Bride):*   And you, _____, place this ring upon your groom's finger as token of wedlock, and repeat these words:

Be thou consecrated unto me with this ring as my husband, according to the faith of God and humanity.

The bride repeats the vow.

OFFICIANT: As by these rings you symbolize your marriage bond, may their meaning sink into your hearts and bind your lives together by devotion and faithfulness to one another. In mutual self-consecration and in ever-deepening love for one another, may you establish a meaningful home among us, a home filled with the spirit of faith, truth, and the fear of God. Praised be Thou, O God, Who sanctifies these Thy children by the holy covenant of marriage.

Pronouncement

117

Benediction

OFFICIANT:

יְבָרֶכְךָ יְיָ וְיִשְׁמְרֶךָ.
יָאֵר יְיָ פָּנָיו אֵלֶיךָ וִיחֻנֶּךָ.
יִשָּׂא יְיָ פָּנָיו אֵלֶיךָ וְיָשֵׂם לְךָ שָׁלוֹם.

May the Lord bless thee and keep thee.
May the Lord let His countenance shine upon thee
and be gracious unto thee.
May the Lord lift up His countenance upon thee and
give thee peace. AMEN.

Notes on the Service

When a Cantor participates in the service, the Call to the Service and the Marriage Blessings are sung. The Welcome Message is not essential. Unlike the Call to the Service, it is usually an informal statement in which the witnesses and guests are welcomed to the wedding. This message may be inserted as an introduction to the reading of Scripture or as a homily.

For an ecumenical service, no indication is made as to how the readings are to be assigned. This is a matter best left to the participants in the service. It would follow, however, that those parts that are unique to a tradition (such as the wine service to the Jewish and the Scriptural readings to the Christian) be read by the representative of that tradition.

The benediction is effectively offered when the rabbi reads the Hebrew text, line by line, and the co-officiant the English.

There is a tendency to split the vow and ring service—with each officiant submitting a vow and offering the ring to the one of his faith. This has the effect of stressing differences, whereas the wedding service should stress the unity of promise and purpose.

See pages 83-90 for a discussion of the symbols of the Jewish wedding service. They may be incorporated into an ecumenical service.

MARRIAGE BETWEEN A CATHOLIC AND AN UNBAPTIZED PERSON

If marriage is celebrated between a Catholic and an unbaptized person, the rite may be performed in the church or some other suitable place and takes the following form.

118

Rite of Welcome and Liturgy of the Word

At the appointed time, the priest, wearing surplice and white stole (or a white cope if desired), proceeds with the ministers to the door of the church or to another appropriate place and greets the bride and the bridegroom.

Where it is desirable that the rite of welcome be omitted, the celebration of marriage begins at once with the liturgy of the word.

The liturgy of the word takes place in the usual manner. There may be three readings, the first of them from the Old Testament. If circumstances make it more desirable, there may be a single reading.

A homily, drawn from the sacred text, is given. It should speak of the obligations of marriage and other appropriate points.

The Service

All stand, including the Bride and the Bridegroom.

PRIEST: My dear friends, you have come together in this church so that the Lord may seal and strengthen your love in the presence of the Church's minister and this community. In this way you will be strengthened to keep mutual and lasting faith with each other and to carry out the other duties of marriage. And so, in the presence of the Church, I ask you to state your intentions.

The priest then questions them about their freedom of choice, faithfulness to each other, and the acceptance and upbringing of children.

PRIEST: _____ and _____, have you come here freely and without reservation to give yourselves to each other in marriage?

Will you love and honor each other as man and wife for the rest of your lives?

Will you accept children lovingly from God, and bring them up according to the law of Christ and His Church?

Each answers the questions separately.

Consent

PRIEST: Since it is your intention to enter into marriage, join your right hands, and declare your consent before God and His Church.

They join hands.

GROOM/BRIDE: I, _____, take you, _____, to be my wife/husband. I promise to be true to you in good times and in bad, in sickness and in health. I will love you and honor you all the days of my life.

If, however, it seems preferable, the priest may obtain consent from the couple through questions.

Weddings

PRIEST *(to Groom/Bride):* _____, do you take _____ to be your wife/husband? Do you promise to be true to her/him in good times and in bad, in sickness and in health, to love her/him and honor her/him all the days of your life?

GROOM/BRIDE: I do.

As in Catholic weddings, other forms may be used.

PRIEST: You have declared your consent before the Church. May the Lord in His goodness strengthen your consent and fill you both with His blessings.
What God has joined, men must not divide. AMEN.

Blessing and Exchange of Rings

PRIEST: May the Lord bless these rings which you give to each other as the sign of your love and fidelity. AMEN.

GROOM/BRIDE: _____, take this ring as a sign of my love and fidelity. In the name of the Father, and of the Son, and of the Holy Spirit.

General Intercessions and Nuptial Blessings

If circumstances so require, the blessing of the bride and bridegroom can be omitted. If used, it is combined with the general intercessions (prayer of the faithful) in this order:

1. First the priest uses the invitatory of any blessing of the couple or any other, taken from any approved formula for the general intercessions.
2. Immediately after the invitatory, there can be either a brief period of silence or a series of petitions from the prayer of the faithful with responses by the people. All the petitions should be in harmony with the blessing that follows, but should not duplicate it.
3. Then, omitting the prayer that concludes the prayer of the faithful, the priest blesses the bride and bridegroom.

Facing them, he joins his hands.

PRIEST: My brothers and sisters, let us ask God for His continued blessings upon this bridegroom and his bride.

All pray silently for a short while. Then the priest extends his hands.

PRIEST: Holy Father, Creator of the Universe,
Maker of man and woman in Your own likeness,
Source of blessing for the married life,
we humbly pray to You for this bride
who today is united with her husband in the bond of marriage.

120

May Your fullest blessing come upon her and her husband
so that they may together rejoice in Your gift of married
     love.
May they be noted for their good lives,
and be parents filled with virtue.
Lord, may they both praise You when they are happy
and turn to You in their sorrows.
May they be glad that You help them in their work,
and know that You are with them in their need.
May they reach old age in the company of their friends,
and come at last to the Kingdom of Heaven.
We ask this through Christ our Lord.
AMEN.

Conclusion of the Celebration

The rite may be concluded with the Lord's Prayer (or, if the nuptial blessing has been omitted, another prayer by the priest) using the customary form, "May almighty God bless you."

A CATHOLIC–JEWISH SERVICE

Introduction (Priest or Rabbi)

The introduction may emphasize the universal spirit of love, the differences inherent in all marriages, or the various attitudes of religious disciplines to the ecumenical marriage service.

Invocation

The traditional Hebrew text may be offered by the rabbi. The text may be read responsively, with the rabbi reading the Hebrew and the Priest responding with the translation.

Scriptural Readings

The inclusion of Scriptural readings is common to Christian services. Lists of appropriate readings are available. A suggested list is included in the chapter on Catholic weddings (see pages 72-73 above). Bride and groom are free to make their own selection and may invite guests to offer the readings.

Exhortation or Homily

The exhortation or homily, properly developed, elaborates upon the theme of marriage and personalizes the service.

121

Prayer of Intercession

This is the recitation of intentions, to which the assembled respond, "Lord, hear our prayer." It is an optional part of the ceremony.

Exchange of Vows

The wordings of vows vary. Often, bride and groom will select or compose their vows. The forms may vary, as noted in the section on the Jewish–Christian service.

Blessing and Exchange of Rings

The blessing of rings is a Christian tradition. For the Jewish experience, historically the ring is that object with which the groom "acquires" the bride. In the contemporary setting, the ring becomes a symbol of the "wholeness" of the impending union. Therefore, it can very well be introduced with a blessing.

For the words spoken in the exchange of rings, see page 74 above.

Wine Service

In this service, two cups of wine are recommended. This follows the traditional Jewish practice of reading the engagement and marriage services consecutively and offering a cup of wine to bride and groom in each of the services.

RABBI: Let this cup of wine symbolize the joys of life you are destined to share. Drink deeply of the cup of joy.

A prayer on marriage and a reading from the biblical book of Hosea may follow.

Confirmation of Marriage Bond

A confirmation may be offered by both the rabbi and the priest.

The Lord's Prayer

This optional part of the service may begin with an introduction by the rabbi and the reading by the priest. It is customary for the congregation to join in the reading.

Benedictions

The Concluding Benediction may be offered by the priest and the Priestly Benediction by the rabbi.

Breaking of the Glass

See page 90 above.

Sign of Peace

Alternate Form of Consent

BRIDE AND GROOM: We believe that by our love we bear witness to the union of God and His people.

We believe that we are meant to be to each other a sign of God's love.

We believe we are called to bring each other to God.

We believe we are called to build upon the family of God here on earth.

We believe that we are meant to give our children in service to God and mankind.

GROOM: I accept you as my wife and call upon the Jewish and Christian communities to witness our union.

BRIDE: With the witness of these communities, we offer ourselves together as husband and wife to God.

WITNESSES: We have heard _____ and _____ pledge themselves to each other and to God in marriage.

Before God and these communities, we testify that _____ and _____ are now husband and wife, one flesh.

AN INNOVATIVE SERVICE

This nondenominational service is an example of one couple's collaborative effort. All or part of it may be incorporated in an ecumenical service.

Processional

Invitation

MINISTER 1: Parents, neighbors, friends: We are gathered here, in God's presence, but in the midst of a divided and broken world, to witness the marriage of these two people who stand before you in love, in trust, and in hope. They ask God to bless their coming together and to sustain them through the years to come. And they ask us to be present with them, rejoice in their oneness, and share in their joy.

MINISTER 2: By our presence here, we undertake the responsibility for supporting _____ and _____ in this deeper relationship into which they are about to enter. We will rejoice in

123

their happiness, support them in times of testing, offer them our patience and forgiveness when they make mistakes, and remember them in our prayers.

Who gives this man in marriage?

CONGREGATION: We do.

MINISTER 1: Who gives this woman in marriage?

CONGREGATION: We do.

Readings

MINISTER 1: *[Recites I Corinthians 1-13.]*

Vows

MINISTER 1: *[Asks for vows.]*

BRIDE/GROOM *repeat the vows:* I, _____, choose you _____, to be my husband/wife as my friend and my love. On this day I affirm the relationship we have enjoyed, looking to the future to keep and strengthen it.

I will be yours in plenty and in want, in sickness and in health, in failure and in triumph.

Together, we will dream, break bread, and lie down; we will stumble but restore each other; we will share all things.

I will cherish and respect you, comfort and encourage you, be open with you, and stay with you as long as we shall live.

MINISTER 2: A good marriage must be created. In the art of marriage the little things are the big things.

MINISTER 1: It is remembering to say "I love you" at least once each day.

It is never going to sleep angry.

It is at no time taking the other for granted; the courtship should not end with the honeymoon, it should continue through all the years.

MINISTER 2: It is having a mutual sense of values and common objectives.

It is standing together facing the world.

It is forming a circle of love that gathers in the whole family.

MINISTER 1: It is doing things for each other, not in the attitude of duty or sacrifice, but in the spirit of joy.

It is speaking words of appreciation and demonstrating gratitude in thoughtful ways.

It is not looking for perfection in each other.

It is cultivating flexibility, patience, understanding, and a sense of humor.

MINISTER 2: It is having the capacity to forgive and forget.
It is giving each other an atmosphere in which each can grow.
It is finding room for things of the spirit.
It is a common search for the good and the beautiful.

MINISTER 1: It is establishing a relationship in which "the independence is equal, the dependence is mutual, and the obligation is reciprocal."

MINISTER 2: *[Homily.]*

Wine Ceremony

MINISTER 2: ...and as you share the cup of wine, so may you share all things from this day on with love and understanding.

[Meditation]

MINISTER 1: These rings are the symbols of the vows here taken; circles of wholeness, perfect in form.

These rings mark the beginning of a long journey together, filled with wonder, surprises, laughter, tears, celebration, grief and joy.

May these rings glow in reflection of the warmth and the lives which flow through the wearers today.

Exchange of Rings

BRIDE/GROOM: I offer you this ring as a sign of my love and fidelity. It shall be a symbol of our vows which have made us husband and wife here today.

I accept this ring as a symbol of our love and wear it proudly as your wife/husband.

[Meditation.]

MINISTER 1: Just as all people need love and support, a marriage cannot exist alone. You, as those closest to _____ and _____, share a responsibility to help provide a wholesome environment to help their marriage grow.

MINISTER 1 and MINISTER 2: *[Pronouncement.]*

Recessional

ANOTHER SERVICE

A service has been prepared and is offered by the clergy of the United Nations Chapel. Following is the text of that service.

OFFICIANT: Good friends of _____ and _____, we welcome you to this Center. We believe that it is God's will that men should beat their swords into plowshares, that they should sit unafraid under their vines and fig trees, and that they should be blessed in peacemaking. Prophet Isaiah expressed the hope of bringing people closer together when he declared: "My House shall be called a House for All Peoples." The Psalmist exclaimed: "Behold how good and pleasant it is for brethren to dwell together in unity" (Psalm 133:1).

Today we have standing together at the altar a bride and a groom who are of different faiths. They symbolize a lesson in love and brotherhood and harmony, admonishing us to seek and find the elements that bring us closer to one another. They believe that there is nothing in their faiths which prevents their marriage. They see each other as objects of love and worthy of the sacrament of marriage. This is a concrete expression of that spirit of human unity which we are seeing manifested so much in this part of the twentieth century between whites and blacks, Protestants and Catholics, Jews and Christians, Marxists and believers.

"This is the day the Lord has made, let us rejoice and be glad in it."

Invocation

OFFICIANT: Blessed be he who comes in the Name of the Lord. We bless you out of the House of the Lord (Psalm 118:26).

O God, supremely blessed,
Supreme in might and glory,
Guide and bless this groom and this bride.

Our God, and God of our Fathers, grant Thy choicest blessing to this groom, _____, and to this bride, _____, who are about to enter the Holy Covenant of Marriage. They seek Thee, O God, out of the joy of their troth that their devotion to each other may gain Thy favor. Hopefully they look forward to the morrow that under Thy protection they may establish a home of their own, filled with the spirit of love, loyalty, faithfulness, commitment, and dedication to each other's happiness and well being.

Teach them, O God, that unless Thou dost build the house, they who build it labor in vain. Hallow their love, bind their lives together, and help them to face the future with faith in one another and with unshakeable confidence in Thy Divine Providence. Guide them through every trial and temptation. In Thy grace, join them unto

126

each other with a love that shall not falter, neither will it fade, and cause them to approach the time-tested, age-old institution of marriage with understanding hearts, courage, confidence, and faith. AMEN.

Readings

OFFICIANT: As we prepare for the solemn and joyful moment when _____ and _____ exchange their marriage vows, it is good for us to reflect thoughtfully on the Scriptures concerning love and marriage.

Then God said: "Let us make man in our image, after our likeness; and let him have dominion over the fish of the sea, and over the birds of the air, and over the cattle, and over all the earth, and over every creeping thing that creeps upon the earth." So, God created man in His own image, in the image of God He created him; male and female He created them. And God blessed them. And God saw everything that He made, and behold, it was very good."

or:

"And I will show you a still more excellent way. If I speak in the tongues of men and of angels, but have not love, I am a noisy gong or a clanging cymbal."

"And if I have prophetic powers, and understand all mysteries and all knowledge, and if I have all faith, so as to remove mountains, but have not love, I gain nothing."

"Love is patient and kind. Love is not jealous or boastful; it is not arrogant or rude. Love does not insist on its own way; it is not irritable or resentful; it does not rejoice at wrong, but rejoices in the right. Love bears all things, believes all things, hopes all things, endures all things. ... So faith, hope, love abide, these three; but the greatest of these is love."

Exhortation

OFFICIANT: This union then is serious, because it will bind you together for life in a relationship so close and so intimate that it will profoundly influence your whole future. That future, with its hopes and disappointments, its success and its failures, its pleasures and its pains, its joys and sorrows, is hidden from your eyes. You know that these elements are mingled in every life and are to be expected in your own. And so, not knowing what is before you, you take each other for better or for worse, for richer or for poorer, in sickness and in health, until death.

Questions for Parents *(Optional)*

OFFICIANT: Mr. and Mrs. _____, your son/daughter _____ wishes to marry _____. In this does he/she have your approval and blessing?

PARENT: Yes.

Intent

OFFICIANT *to Bride and Groom:* _____, do you wish to have _____ as your husband/wife?

BRIDE/GROOM: I do.

OFFICIANT *to Bride and Groom:* _____, I take you to be my husband/wife. I promise to be true to you in good times and in bad, in sickness and in health. I will love you and honor you all the days of my life.

Bride and Groom repeat phrase by phrase.

Blessing and Exchange of Rings

OFFICIANT: Heavenly Father, may it be good in Thy sight to bless these rings. May they bring joy, gladness, happiness and harmony to bride and groom in the holy wedlock of matrimony.

Dear _____, with this ring I thee wed, and by it be thou consecrated unto me, as my wedded wife/husband according to the laws of God and man.

Groom and Bride repeat.

Confirmation of the Wedding Bond

OFFICIANT: Forasmuch as you, _____ and _____, have consented together in holy wedlock, and therefore have pledged your faith to each other, by the authority of the Church I ratify and bless the bond of marriage which you have contracted. AMEN.

or:

This Interfaith Marriage Ceremony is drawing to its conclusion. I join in ratifying the confirmation of your marriage vows. And I am doing so by the virtue of the ecclesiastical authority vested in me at the time of my ordination. Therefore, I do hereby declare your marriage to be valid and binding, and I do hereby pronounce you, _____, and you, _____, to be husband and wife in the sight of God and man. AMEN.

128

Benediction

OFFICIANT: May the Lord lift His countenance upon you and grant you the blessings of peace and of health and happiness and harmony—with each other, with your loved ones, with your fellowmen, and with your God—now and forevermore. AMEN.

The Orthodox Christian Wedding

Marriage, for the Orthodox Christian, is a sacrament, a meeting of two beings in love, a human love which can be transformed by the sacramental grace of the Holy Spirit into an eternal bond, indissoluble even by death.

An Orthodox Christian wedding takes place in a church. Under exceptional circumstances, with the permission of the Bishop, the wedding may take place elsewhere. A wedding normally takes place during the morning hours, preferably following the morning liturgy. The bride and groom fast prior to the ceremony. In contemporary practice, however, a wider latitude is permitted in establishing the time for a wedding. The times when weddings are not scheduled are the Lenten season; the Advent and Epiphany seasons, i.e., from the beginning of Christmas Advent (November 28th) to the Feast of the Epiphany (January 6th); the Fasting season preceding both the Feast of Saints Peter and Paul (in June) and the Feast of the Dormition (in August); and special one-day fast periods.

A couple desiring to be married should meet with their pastor to learn more about the sacrament of marriage as well as its problems and promises. They should also present to him their baptism and chrismation certificates. Satisfied that the marriage will receive the blessings of all concerned, the pastor permits the announcement of the marriage banns. It includes the names of bride and groom and their respective places of birth, names of parents and their residence. The announcement is repeated on three occasions during the Sunday or holy day Divine Liturgy.

Prior to the wedding, preferably on that day, the bride and groom approach the confessional and partake of the Sacrament of Penance and then Holy Communion in order that they cleanse themselves of all sin and come pure before the marriage altar. A woman who is marrying for the first time should wear a white gown. The groomsman, or best man, must be of the Orthodox faith. Other witnesses, ushers, and bridesmaids may be non-Orthodox.

Although second or successive marriages are sanctioned, they are not considered to be fully sacramental, but rather marriages blessed by the Orthodox Church as a condescension to human weakness, with the prayers in the "Order for a Second Marriage" being penitential in character.

The Wedding Service

For the wedding service, a sacramental table is arranged and placed directly in front of the Sanctuary. The table should contain candles, the Book of the Gospels, hand cross, wreaths (crowns), wine, and a sprinkler with holy water. If icons are to be presented to bride and groom, they should be placed on the table.

The service is in two parts, the Betrothal and the Crowning (marriage service). The Betrothal dramatizes the free decision made by the bride and groom and is symbolized by the giving of rings. This service begins at the door of the church and is completed before the altar. The marriage service begins immediately thereafter, culminating in the crowning of the groom and bride. The following is a description of the Orthodox Christian wedding.

The Betrothal. The bride, groom, and their attendants gather in the vestibule at the entrance to the church. The priest comes forward to meet them. The bride and groom stand before the priest, the groom to the right of the bride.

> PRIEST: Have you a good, free, and unconstrained will and a firm intention to take as wife/husband this woman/man who you see before you?
>
> GROOM/BRIDE: I do.
>
> PRIEST: Have you not promised yourself to any other woman/man in matrimony?
>
> GROOM/BRIDE: No.

The priest then bids the groom and bride, followed by their attendants, to enter the church and stand before the altar.

Two rings are essential to the service. In contemporary practice, both rings are gold. The rings are blessed and placed on the fourth finger of the right hand of the groom and the bride.

In the ritual of the Carpatho-Russian Orthodox service, the bride and groom then kneel and place their right hands upon the Book of the Gospels, forming a cross with the groom's hand over his bride's. The priest places a portion of his vestment (the *Epitrachil*) over the crossed hands and calls for the recitation of the nuptial vows.

> GROOM/BRIDE: I, _____, take you, _____, as my wedded wife/husband, and I promise you love, honor, and respect; to be faithful to you and not to forsake you until death do us part. So help me God, one in the Holy Trinity, and all the Saints.

The Crowning. The wreaths used in the Crowning are varied. They may be green wreaths, decorated metal crowns, flowers, or olive leaves.

The crown is referred to as the "Martyr's Crown." The word "martyr" means "witness." Its messages are varied: an eternal witness of the union of Christ with the Church into which groom and bride are being welcomed and united; a royal reward for preserving purity of body before marriage; a keeping holy of wedded life; victory over passion.

In placing the crown on the groom's head, the priest makes the sign of the cross three times and says:

> PRIEST: The servant of God is crowned to the handmaid of God in the name of the Father, and of the Son, and of the Holy Spirit.

He repeats the ritual for the bride and then says:

> PRIEST: Lord, our God, crown them with glory and honor.

The service then continues with the readings of the Gospel and Epistle, followed by a Litany and its responses. During the Litany, a cup of wine may be offered to the groom and bride with the invocation: "O Lord, Who has created all things, bless _____ and _____ now with Your spiritual blessing, this Common Cup, which is given to them who are now united in the community of marriage." The priest gives the cup to the groom and then to the bride. They drink. In a Greek tradition, bread is dipped into the wine and then given to the bride and groom.

The wine recalls the Gospel story of the Marriage in Cana, where, it is said, the Lord changed the vats of water into wine. The single cup from which groom and bride partake symbolizes sharing the joys and trials in wedded life.

The priest leads groom and bride in a circle around the tetrapod three times. They are followed by the groomsman and bridesmaid, who carry the crowns above the couple's heads. The circle symbolizes the eternal aspect of marriage with the Trinity, witness to their marriage.

Following a benediction, the priest may lead the bride to an icon of the Virgin Mother. She kneels before the icon while the priest intones a special prayer and sprinkles the bride with holy water. The bride may bring a bouquet of flowers with her and place it before the icon. In some services, gift of icons are presented to the bride and groom.

From Veil to Babushka

The bride wears a veil during the wedding service and during the reception that follows. A folk custom calls for a special time during the reception, when, with dance, the women lift the bride's veil, take it from her, and replace it with a "babushka," symbolizing the transition from girl to woman.

Validity of a Mixed Marriage

The Catholic Church has decreed that a marriage that takes place between an Orthodox Christian and a non-Orthodox Christian is valid in the eyes of the Catholic Church. For additional information on mixed marriage, see the section "Orthodox Christian Attitude Toward Interfaith Marriage" in the chapter on "Interfaith Weddings" (page 112).

The Carpatho-Russian Orthodox Wedding

The following service is adapted from *The Ritual of the Sacrament of Holy Matrimony,* compiled by The Very Reverend Elias Kozar, Protopresbyter, St. Mary's Carpatho-Russian Orthodox Greek Catholic Church, Yonkers, N.Y. Used with permission.

Betrothal Service

PRIEST: *[Psalm 127.]*
Blessed is everyone who fears the Lord, who walks in His ways. You shall eat of the fruit of your labors; blessed are you, and it shall be well with you.

CHOIR: Glory to Thee, our God. Glory to Thee!

PRIEST: Your wife shall be like a fruitful vine, within your house; your children like young olive plants around your table. Behold in this way shall the man be blessed who fears the Lord.

CHOIR: Glory to Thee, our God. Glory to Thee!

PRIEST: The Lord shall bless you out of Zion, and you shall see the good things of Jerusalem all the days of your life. That you may see your children's children. Peace upon Israel!

CHOIR: Glory to Thee, our God. Glory to Thee!

134

PRIEST *to Groom/Bride:* Have you, _____, a good, free and uncon-
strained will and a firm intention to take unto yourself
_____, here present, to be your wife/husband?

GROOM/BRIDE: I have.

PRIEST: You have not promised matrimonial faithfulness to another?

GROOM/BRIDE: I have not.

PRIEST: Blessed is the Kingdom of the Father, and of the Son, and of
the Holy Spirit, now and ever, and forever.

CHOIR: AMEN.

PRIEST: In peace let us pray to the Lord.

CHOIR: Lord, have mercy.

PRIEST: For the servants of God, _____ and _____, who are now
being united to each other in the community of marriage, and
for their salvation, let us pray to the Lord.

CHOIR: Lord, have mercy.

PRIEST: That He will bless this marriage, as He blessed that in Cana of
Galilee, let us pray to the Lord.

CHOIR: Lord, have mercy.

PRIEST: That He will grant unto them chastity, and of the fruit of the
womb as is expedient for them, let us pray to the Lord.

CHOIR: Lord, have mercy.

PRIEST: That He will make them glad with the sight of sons and daughters, let us pray to the Lord.

CHOIR: Lord, have mercy.

PRIEST: That He will grant unto them the procreation of virtuous offspring, and an upright life, let us pray to the Lord.

CHOIR: Lord, have mercy.

PRIEST: That He will grant to them and to us all petitions, which are unto salvation, let us pray to the Lord.

CHOIR: Lord, have mercy.

PRIEST: That they and we be delivered from all affliction, wrath, and
want, let us pray to the Lord.

CHOIR: Lord, have mercy.

PRIEST: Help us, save us, have mercy on us and protect us, O God, by
Your grace.

CHOIR: Lord, have mercy.

PRIEST: Commemorating our most holy, most pure, most blessed and
glorious Lady, the Birth-Giver of God and Ever-Virgin Mary,
with all the Saints, let us commend ourselves and each other
and all our life to Christ, our God.

135

CHOIR: To You, O Lord.

PRIEST: For to You are due all glory, honor and adoration, to the Father, and to the Son, and to the Holy Spirit, now and ever, and forever.

CHOIR: AMEN.

PRIEST: Let us pray to the Lord.

CHOIR: Lord, have mercy.

PRIEST: O God, most pure, Creator of every living thing, Who did transform the rib of our forefather Adam into a wife, because of Your love towards mankind; and did bless them saying unto them, "Increase and multiply and have dominion over the earth"; and did make of the two one flesh, for which cause a man shall leave his father and mother and cleave unto his wife, and the two shall be one flesh, and whom God has joined together, let no man put asunder. You blessed your servant Abraham, and opening the womb of Sarah, made him to be the father of many nations; You gave Isaac to Rebecca and blessed her in childbearing; You joined Jacob unto Rachel and from that union made known the twelve Patriarchs; You united Joseph with Asenath, giving unto them as the fruit of their procreation Ephraim and Manasses; You accepted Zacharias and Elizabeth, and declared their offspring to be the Forerunner: from the Root of Jesse, according to the flesh, blossomed forth the Ever-Virgin Mary and You were incarnate and born of her for the redemption of the human race; through Your indescribable gift and great goodness, You came to Cana of Galilee and blessed the marriage there, that You might make manifest that it is Your will that there should be lawful marriage and the begetting of children therefrom.

We entreat You, the same all holy Master: Accept the prayer of us, Your servants, and as You were present there, so likewise be present here with Your invisible protection. Bless this marriage and grant unto these Your servants, _____ and _____, a peaceful life, length of days, matrimonial chastity, mutual love in the bond of peace, long-lived posterity, gratitude from their children, a crown of glory that does not fade away. Graciously grant that they may behold their children's children. Keep their married life above reproach, and give them of the dew of heaven from on high, and of the fatness of the earth. Fill their houses with wheat and wine and oil, and with every beneficence, that they may bestow in turn upon the needy; granting also unto those who are here present with them all those petitions which are for their salvation. For You are the God of mercy, and bounties, and love toward mankind,

136

and unto You do we give glory, together with Your eternal Father and Your most holy, gracious, and life-giving Spirit, now and ever, and forever.

CHOIR: AMEN.

PRIEST: Let us pray to the Lord.

The Priest blesses the two rings with Holy Water.

CHOIR: Lord, have mercy.

PRIEST: O Lord, our God, Who has espoused the Church as a pure Virgin from among the Gentiles: Bless this Betrothal, and unite and maintain these Your servants in peace and oneness of mind. For unto You are due all glory, honor and worship, to the Father, and to the Son, and to the Holy Spirit, now and ever, and forever.

CHOIR: AMEN.

The Priest blesses the bridal pair, making the sign of the cross with the rings, and then places the rings on the ring finger of the right hand of the Groom and of the Bride.

PRIEST *to Groom/Bride:* The servant of God, _____, is betrothed to the servant of God, _____, in the name of the Father, and of the Son, and of the Holy Spirit. AMEN.

The Marriage Vows

The Groom and Bride kneel down, join their right hands upon the Book of Gospels. The Priest places the Epitrachil *upon their joined hands, holds it in place with his right hand, and then says:*

PRIEST *to Groom/Bride:* Repeat after me:

I, _____, take you, _____, as my wedded wife/husband, and I promise you love, honor, and respect; to be faithful to you, and not to forsake you until death do us part. So help me God, one in the Holy Trinity, and all the Saints.

The Groom and Bride repeat the vows. The Priest removes the Epitrachil *from over the hands of the Groom and Bride; the Groom and Bride in turn separate their hands, but keep them on the Book of the Gospels; the Priest then blesses them with the sign of the cross, reciting the following prayer.*

PRIEST: What God has joined together, let no man put asunder; and, therefore, I, an unworthy servant of God, through the power given unto me, do unite you in Holy Matrimony, and by virtue of the authority of the Holy Orthodox Church do affirm and signify this: In the name of the Father, and of the Son, and of the Holy Spirit. AMEN.

The Groom and Bride rise and kiss the Book of Gospels, after which the Priest gives to each a lighted candle to hold.

PRIEST: Let us pray to the Lord.

CHOIR: Lord, have mercy.

PRIEST: O holy God, Who created man out of dust, and fashioned his wife out of his rib, and joined her unto him as a helpmate, for it seemed good to Your Majesty that man should not be alone upon the earth. Now, O Master, stretch forth Your hand from Your holy dwelling-place, and join these Your servants, _____ and _____, for by You is the wife joined to her husband. Unite them in one mind, wed them into one flesh, granting unto them of the fruit of the body and the procreation of good children. For Yours is the majesty, and Yours are the kingdom and the power and the glory, of the Father, and of the Son, and of the Holy Spirit, now and ever, and forever.

CHOIR: AMEN.

The Crowning

The Priest crowns first the Groom and then the Bride, saying over each:

PRIEST: The servant of God, _____, is crowned unto the servant of God, _____, in the name of the Father, and of the Son, and of the Holy Spirit. AMEN.

And blessing the couple, the Priest says:

PRIEST: O Lord, Our God, crown them with glory and honor.

Prokimen

PRIEST: Let us be attentive! Peace be unto all! Wisdom, be attentive!

READER: The Prokimen....Thou hast set upon their heads crowns of precious stones; they asked life of Thee, and Thou gave it to them. (Tone 8). *Verse:* For Thou will give them Thy blessing forever and ever: Thou will make them rejoice with gladness through Thy presence.

Epistle

PRIEST: Wisdom!

READER: *[Reads The Reading from the Epistle of Saint Paul the Apostle to the Ephesians (5: 20-33).]*

PRIEST: Let us be attentive!

READER: Brethren: Give thanks always for all things, in the name of our Lord Jesus Christ to God the Father; being subject one to another, in the fear of Christ. Let women be subject to their husbands, as to the Lord. For the husband is the head of the wife, as Christ is the head of the Church and He is the Savior of the body. Therefore, as the Church is subject to Christ, so also let the wives be to their husbands in all things. Husbands, love your wives, as Christ also loved the Church and delivered Himself up for it; that He might sanctify it having cleansed it by the washing of water with the Word; that He might present it to Himself a glorious Church, not having spot or wrinkle, or any such thing, but that it should be holy and without blemish. So also ought men to love their wives as their own bodies. He that loves his wife, loves himself. For no man ever hates his own flesh, but nourishes and cherishes it, as Christ does the Church, because we are members of His body, of His flesh, and of His bones. "For this reason shall a man leave his father and mother and shall be joined to his wife, and the two shall become one flesh." This is a great mystery; but I speak concerning Christ and the Church. However, let everyone of you love his wife as himself, and let the wife respect her husband.

PRIEST: Peace be with you. Wisdom! Be Attentive!

CHOIR: Alleluja. Alleluja. Alleluja.

PRIEST: Wisdom! Be attentive, as we listen to the Holy Gospel! Peace be unto all!

CHOIR: And with Your spirit.

PRIEST: *[Reads The Reading of the Holy Gospel according to Saint John (2: 1-11).]*

CHOIR: Glory to You, O Lord, Glory to You!

PRIEST: Let us be attentive!

At that time, there was a marriage in Cana of Galilee, and the mother of Jesus was there. And Jesus was also invited, with His disciples to the marriage. When there was no more wine, the mother of Jesus said to Him: "They have no wine." And Jesus said to her: "Woman, what is that to me and to you? My hour has not yet come." His mother said to the servants: "Whatsover He shall say to you, do it." Now six stone jars were standing there, for the Jewish rites of purification, each holding twenty or thirty gallons. Jesus said to them: "Fill the jars with water." And they filled them up to the brim. And Jesus said to them: "Now draw some out, and take it to the steward of the feast." And they took it. And when the steward had tasted the water made wine, and did not know where it came from, but the servants who had drawn the water knew, the steward of the feast called the bridegroom and said to him: "Every man at first sets forth the good wine, and when men have well drunk, then that which is of lesser quality is served. But you have kept the good wine until now." This, the first of His signs, Jesus did in Cana of Galilee, and manifested His glory; and His disciples believed in Him.

CHOIR: Glory to You, O Lord, Glory to You.

Litany

PRIEST: Let us all say with our whole soul and with our whole mind, let us say.

CHOIR: Lord, have mercy.

PRIEST: O Lord Almighty, God of our fathers, we pray to You, hear us and have mercy.

CHOIR: Lord, have mercy.

PRIEST: Have mercy on us, O God, according to Your great mercy. We pray to You, hear us and have mercy.

CHOIR: Lord, have mercy. Lord, have mercy. Lord, have mercy.

PRIEST: Furthermore we pray for the health and salvation of the servants of God, _____ and _____, now united to each other in marriage.

CHOIR: Lord, have mercy. Lord, have mercy. Lord, have mercy.

PRIEST: Furthermore, we pray for the people present in this Holy Church, who await Your great and abundant mercy, for those who have shown us mercy and for all Christians, for their health and salvation.

CHOIR: Lord, have mercy. Lord, have mercy. Lord, have mercy.

PRIEST: For You are a merciful God Who loves mankind, and we give glory to You, to the Father, and to the Son, and to the Holy Spirit, now and ever, and forever.

CHOIR: AMEN.

PRIEST: And make us worthy, O Lord, that we may with full confidence and without condemnation dare to call upon You, God Our Heavenly Father, and say unto You:

CHOIR or CONGREGATION: Our Father, Who art in Heaven, Hallowed be Thy Name. Thy kingdom come. Thy will be done on earth, as it is in heaven. Give us this day our daily bread. And forgive us our trespasses, as we forgive those who trespass against us. And lead us not into temptation, but deliver us from evil.

PRIEST: For Thine is the kingdom, and the power, and the glory, of the Father and of the Son, and of the Holy Spirit, now and ever, and forever.

CHOIR: AMEN.

PRIEST: Peace be unto all.

CHOIR: And with Your Spirit.

PRIEST: Let us bow our heads unto the Lord.

CHOIR: To You, O Lord.

The Priest blesses the Common Cup.

PRIEST: Let us pray to the Lord.

CHOIR: Lord, have mercy.

PRIEST: O God, Who has created all things by Your might, and established the universe, and Who has adorned the crown of all things created by You: Bless now with Your spiritual blessing this Common Cup, which is given to them who are now united in the community of marriage.

Taking the cup of wine, the Priest gives it to drink first to the Groom and then to the Bride, three times.

PRIEST: For blessed is Your Name, and glorified is Your kingdom, of the Father, and of the Son, and of the Holy Spirit, now and ever, and forever.

CHOIR: AMEN.

Immediately after the ceremony of the Common Cup, the Priest leads the Groom and Bride around the Tetrapod three times, with the best man and the maid-of-honor (or the groomsmen) following behind the bridal couple and holding the crowns above the heads of the Groom and Bride.

CHOIR: Rejoice, O Isaiah! A Virgin is with Child, and shall bear a Son, Emmanuel, both God and Man: And Orient is His Name, Whom magnifying, we call the Virgin Blessed. O Holy Martyrs, who fought the good fight and have received your crowns, entreat the Lord that He will have mercy on our souls.

Glory to You, O Christ God, the Apostles' boast, the Martyrs' joy, who proclaimed the consubstantial Trinity.

The Priest removes the crown of the Groom.

PRIEST: Be exalted, O Bridegroom, as Abraham; and be blessed as Isaac; and multiply like Jacob, walking in peace, and keeping the commandments of God in righteousness.

Then the Priest removes the crown of the Bride.

PRIEST: And you, O Bride, be exalted as Sarah; and be joyful as Rebecca; and multiply like Rachel, rejoicing in your husband and observing the provisions of the law, for so it is well pleasing unto God.

Let us pray to the Lord.

CHOIR: Lord, have mercy.

PRIEST: O God, our God, Who came to Cana of Galilee and blessed the Marriage there, Bless also these Your servants, who through Your providence are now united together in wedlock. Bless the daily course of their lives; fill their life with good things; and receive their crowns into Your kingdom, preserving them pure, blameless, and above reproach, forever and ever.

CHOIR: AMEN.

PRIEST: Peace be unto all!

CHOIR: And with Your spirit.

PRIEST: Let us bow our heads unto the Lord.

CHOIR: To You, O Lord.

PRIEST: May the Father, and the Son, and the Holy Spirit, the all-holy, consubstantial and life-creating Trinity, One Godhead and Kingdom, bless you and grant you a long life and good children: That you might advance in life and in faith and that you might be filled with an abundance of all earthly good things. May you be deemed worthy of receiving the promised blessings through the prayers of the holy Birth-giver of God, and of all the Saints.

CHOIR: AMEN.

The Priest leads the Bride to the icon of the Mother of God, before which the Bride kneels, and the Priest then intones the following prayer, during which he bestows a blessing upon the Bride.

PRIEST: Let us pray to the Lord.

CHOIR: Lord, have mercy.

PRIEST: O God, our God, Who spoke through the Prophets and declared in advance that in the last days all nations will come to the light of Your knowledge, and not wishing that any man created by You should be without participation in Your salvation, through the Apostle Paul, Your chosen vessel, You have given a law to men and women living in faith, to do everything for Your glory: to men that they should with uncovered head bring praise and glory to Your most holy Name; to women, that they in piety and purity, being resolute in their good deeds and strengthened in the faith, with covered head should gratefully bring praises and prayers to Your glory. Now, O merciful Lord, bless this Your servant, _____, and adorn her head with the beauty pleasing to You, that living according to Your laws, and progressing to Your satisfaction in all the virtues, she may preserve herself in matrimonial chastity, and together with her husband, given to her by You, she may receive eternal happiness. For You are a merciful God, Who loves mankind, and to You we give glory, to the Father, and to the Son, and to the Holy Spirit, now and ever, and forever.

CHOIR: AMEN.

The Priest then raises his hand in a blessing over the Bride's head.

PRIEST: May the Lord protect you with the shadow of His wings, and preserve you from all manner of evil during all the days of your life, and grant you to see in peace and happiness the sons of your sons down to the third and fourth generation together with your husband.

By the sprinkling of this holy water may the blessing of the Father and of the Son and of the Holy Spirit descend and remain upon you. AMEN.

Dismissal

PRIEST: Wisdom!

CHOIR: More honorable than the Cherubim and beyond compare more glorious than the Seraphim, who as a Virgin gave birth to God the Word, true Birth-giver of God, we magnify you.

PRIEST: Glory to You, O Chirst, our God, our hope, Glory to You!

CHOIR: Glory to the Father, and to the Son, and to the Holy Spirit, now and ever, and forever. AMEN.

Lord, have mercy. Lord, have mercy. Lord, have mercy. Father, give the Blessing!

PRIEST: May Christ, our true God, Who by His presence at the Marriage Feast in Cana of Galilee declared marriage to be honorable; through the prayers of His most pure Mother, to whom this Church is reverently dedicated; of the holy, glorious and all-praiseworthy Apostles; of the holy, God-crowned Kings and Equal-to-the-Apostles Constantine and Helena; of the holy Great Martyr Procopius; and of all the Saints, have mercy on us and save us, for He is good and loves mankind.

CHOIR: AMEN.

The Cross is venerated by the Groom and the Bride with the following greeting and response.

PRIEST: Christ is among us!

RESPONSE: He is and ever shall be!

PRIEST: Grant, O Lord, to Your servants, _____ and _____, united this day in the Sacrament of Marriage, spiritual peace, good health and happiness, for many and blessed years!

CHOIR: God grant them many years! God grant them many years! God grant them many, many and blessed years!

143

The Muslim Wedding

Marriage for the Muslim is the better way of life. The Qur'an, God's Word to His believers, reads: "He has created mates for you from yourselves that you might find quiet of mind in them, and He put between you love and compassion."

In ancient practice, a groom was forbidden to see his bride until the hour of the wedding. Likewise, the bride was forbidden to cast eyes upon her groom before the appointed time. In contemporary times, within the tradition, in order to assure the marriage of domestic tranquility, it is recommended that ways be found, prior to the agreement for marriage, for the couple to catch a glimpse of each other discreetly and clandestinely. Still, no private meeting is allowed, for the Prophet has said: "A man and a woman never meet alone except that Satan becomes the third party." In Western societies a groom courts his bride as is the general custom.

Marriage is forbidden between a Muslim and an "idol worshipper"; that is, a Muslim woman and a non-Muslim man. A male Muslim may marry a non-Muslim woman of a faith of which it is said it is of God's revelation, such as the Christian and Jewish faiths.

According to Islamic law, a child of a Muslim is Muslim and is to be reared in the faith.

The Formal Betrothal—*Khitbah*

A prospective groom sends word to the father of his intended bride stating his intentions and requesting permission for a visit, at which time he will bring with him members of his family and friends. During the visit he (or his surrogate, a father, brother, or friend) makes a formal statement regarding his intentions in the following words:

> Praise and gratitude are due to God. We seek His help and forgiveness. May He accept our repentance and protect us against evil desires and wrong deeds. Whoever is guided by God cannot go astray and whoever is abandoned by God, no one can lead him aright. I bear witness there is no God but God and that Muhammad is His servant and messenger.
>
> I have come to ask for the hand of your daughter for myself [or, in the case of a surrogate, my son, brother, etc.].

The bride's family, through their representative, acknowledges the request, following the established form of first reciting a prayer, as above, and then noting its acceptance. Thereupon gifts are presented to the intended bride, customarily now an engagement ring and (as the situation recommends) additional gifts.

Marriage Contract

A contract is drawn between groom and bride and properly witnessed. The contract may be drawn by bride and groom, acting in their own interests, or by agents or representatives of each. Once the contract is drawn and properly witnessed, the parties thereto are bound to each other in accordance with canonical law.

The Marriage—*Aqd an-Nikah*

In Muslim countries a marriage service is performed by a marriage registrar *(ma'dhun)*. In the United States, in keeping with the general practice of the law, it is performed by a clergyperson.

The Place for the Marriage

Preferably, a Muslim wedding is planned for a mosque. However, there are no restrictions upon places other than a mosque.

Witnesses to the Marriage

Witnesses are required for a marriage and are to be Muslim in faith. However, if the bride is not a Muslim, the witnesses need not be Muslim.

The Wedding

The wedding celebrates the consummation of marriage on the part of bride and groom. Family and friends feast for a day or more, depending upon varying traditions. The evening of the wedding day is called *Lailat al-Hinna* (The Henna Night) after the custom of covering the hands and feet of bride and groom with henna. The wedding day is called *Lailat al-Farah* (The Night of Pleasure). Bride and groom do not share in the family celebration. Secluded in their quarters, special foods are sent to them, referred to as the "Mutual Meal."

The Ceremony

Guests and witnesses are seated as are bride and groom, who face each other and clasp their right hands, over which a white cloth may be placed.

An opening prayer is offered by the officiant followed by an inquiry addressed first to the bride, then to the groom, as to their intent one for another. The bride responds.

> BRIDE: I, _____, offer you myself in marriage in accordance with the instructions of the Holy Qur'an and the Holy Prophet, peace and blessing be upon Him.

Since the contract drawn between bride and groom may include special commitments or conditions, in the bride's response, accordingly, words such as "in accordance with the terms of the agreement we entered into" may be added to the response. The groom is questioned and responds in like manner.

Again the officiant addresses bride and groom, this time asking them to pledge their obedience and faithfulness to each other in the following words.

> BRIDE: I pledge, in honesty and with sincerity, to be for you an obedient and faithful wife.
>
> GROOM: I pledge, in honesty and sincerity, to be for you a faithful and helpful husband.

The ceremony is in fact concluded. However, the officiant may convey his wishes, and the prayerful wishes of the assembled, as a concluding note to the ceremony.

Customs

During the wedding (celebration), as the bride is escorted to her new residence, the place of her bridegroom, candy and rice are showered upon her, first to ward off evil spirits that traditionally lurk among celebrants and then to encourage fertility.

Not only do bride and groom receive gifts, but they present gifts to their guests in the form of candy or eggs, attractively prepared as befits the occasion.

Service of Renewal

When a ship sets sail, family and friends of passengers gather to celebrate its departure with abandoned gaiety, giving little or no thought as to how the ship might fare on its journey. Will it arrive safely? Will the purpose of the trip, as individually anticipated, be fulfilled? When the ship returns, there is no fanfare. The ship steals silently into port. Should not the practice be in reverse? Leave in apprehensive silence and return to the welcome sounds of music, the shower of confetti, and the usual libations offered in times of thanksgiving.

When a couple is sent off in marriage, there is rejoicing, even though beneath the layers of celebration there is an inescapable fear and apprehension as to the fate of the marriage. How will the couple fare in life's significant and sacred adventure? After years of weaving their lives together, hardly a word is spoken—certainly no celebration comparable to that of the wedding day. Why not celebrate the fulfillment of the promises made? Some do!

They invite family and friends and share with them in a marriage of renewal. During the ceremony, a statement is made about marriage in general, about their marriage, and about the love that matured since they first gave themselves to each other through the succession of all of love's experiences.

Of the renewal celebrations I have now witnessed, only one has taken place in a sanctuary. It followed the classical form of a wedding with minor changes in the readings to reflect the nature of the service. Another celebration took place in a home. The husband and wife addressed the assembled, telling them why they chose to renew their vows, and in so doing, relived the highlights of their shared experiences. Following their remarks and prior to the conclusion of the

147

service, guests, one by one, rose to speak and tell of their association with the couple, and attest to their friendship and their love with them. A third renewal service took place in the suite of a hotel. Husband and wife stood together, flanked by children, grandchildren, and friends, and shared in a service prepared for them. A table was set up as an altar upon which there were placed several items—some of sentimental significance and others that were used as symbols in the service.

The renewal may be celebrated as part of a church or synagogue service. Since there is no service established for this purpose, the following forms and texts are suggested for those who would plan a Wedding of Renewal.

The Service

OFFICIANT: Here among family and friends, _____ and _____ have asked that we pause with them for a brief and precious moment, as they look back in grateful reminiscence upon the years since first they gave their hearts to each other and to share with them in a prayer of thanksgiving for all that has come to pass, and a prayer of hope for all that is yet to be.

To Husband and Wife: Remembering your vows of yesteryear, made with some apprehension, now in blessed fulfillment, reaffirm your need for and devotion to each other.

HUSBAND/WIFE: Blessed with you, _____, I give thanks to God for our togetherness through all these years which has enriched our lives beyond measure, and promise again with all my heart to love you and to cherish you all the days of our lives.

A Prayer

OFFICIANT: Praised be Thou, O Lord our God, Ruler of the World, Who in Thy mercy makest light to shine over the earth and all its inhabitants, and renewest daily the work of creation. How manifold are Thy works, O Lord! In wisdom hast Thou made them all. The heavens declare Thy glory. The earth reveals Thy creative power. Thou formest light and darkness, ordainest good out of evil, bringest harmony into nature and peace to the heart of man.*

To You, God and Father, we lift our souls in praise, You Who established for us the changing seasons: the palette

---

*Those desirous of including the Hebrew may find the text in the "Notes on the Service" below.

of Fall, its endless range of green fading into the starkness
of Winter and the sudden burst of the vibrancy of Spring
languishing into Summer serenity—telling us of a constant renewal, of a beauty that emerges, grows, changes,
and is always becoming. Help _____ and _____, we
pray to You, to make their years of togetherness seasons of
renewal of love for life, for beauty, for one another. Sanctify this covenant which _____ and _____ have consummated in Your name. Bestow upon them Your gifts of
friendship, of love, and of peace. Let there always be a
sweetness in their family and among their friends. Be with
them at this hour of their gladness; bless this, their covenant; and seal this, their bond, with love everlasting.

A cup of wine is lifted as the blessing is read.

OFFICIANT: Praise be given to You, Master of our destiny, You Who
created the fruit of the vine.*

Husband and wife share the cup of wine.

OFFICIANT: As together you now drink from this cup of wine, so may
you together, under God's guidance, in perfect union and
devotion to each other, continue to draw contentment,
comfort and felicity from the cup of life, and thereby may
you find life's joys doubly gladdening and its bitterness
sweetened by true companionship and love.

Homily

In order to both personalize and enrich the renewal experience, the
officiant may wish to express some thoughts on the subject of renewal or remembrance of things that augur well for the future.

The Giving of Rings

If new ring(s) are used, the following may be read.

OFFICIANT: In the beginning there was the engagement ring, a promise
for that which was to be. Then there came the wedding
band, a commitment made to one another, to love and to
cherish until the end of days. Now comes the ring of renewal, to tell of the trials and the goodness that came to be and
the joys that will yet be. Take this ring, _____, and place
it upon _____'s finger, and as you do so, repeat these
words:

*Those desirous of including the Hebrew may find the text in the "Notes on the Ser-
vice" below.

Weddings

With this ring I reaffirm my love for you, a love refined in the crucible of our togetherness. Wear it as my prayer of thanksgiving and of my hopes for all our tomorrows.

If the original wedding rings are used, the following may be read.

OFFICIANT: Take the rings with which once you did bind your lives together, rings now sanctified by the years of your togetherness. Invest in them the gratefulness of your hearts, and again offer them one to another, repeating with me these words:

With this ring I reaffirm my love for you, a love refined in the crucible of our togetherness. Wear it as my prayer of thanksgiving and of my hopes for all our tomorrows.

The vow is repeated. The recipient responds.

WIFE/HUSBAND: You are mine, my love, and I am yours, so ordained aforetime by our God and Father. We give thanks to Him Who imbued us with the ennobling impulse of love that has brought and kept us together and given us reason to rejoice as we renew our pledge to one another—to love and be loved, to cherish and be cherished all the days of our lives. Be now and forever consecrated to me as my gift and my blessing for life.

OFFICIANT: With these rings and the words you have spoken, you symbolize the renewal of your marriage. May their meaning sink into your hearts and ever more intensely bind your lives together in devotion one to another. Praise be given to You our God Who has sanctified these Thy children, _____ and _____, by the holy covenant of marriage.

Benediction

Notes on the Service

The following Hebrew texts are included here for those of the Jewish faith.

Prayer following the vows:

הַמֵּאִיר לָאָרֶץ וְלַדָּרִים עָלֶיהָ בְּרַחֲמִים, וּבְטוּבוֹ מְחַדֵּשׁ בְּכָל־יוֹם תָּמִיד מַעֲשֵׂה בְרֵאשִׁית. מָה רַבּוּ מַעֲשֶׂיךָ, יְיָ. כֻּלָּם בְּחָכְמָה עָשִׂיתָ. מָלְאָה הָאָרֶץ קִנְיָנֶךָ. תִּתְבָּרַךְ, יְיָ אֱלֹהֵינוּ, עַל־שֶׁבַח מַעֲשֵׂה יָדֶיךָ. וְעַל־מְאוֹרֵי־אוֹר שֶׁעָשִׂיתָ יְפָאֲרוּךָ סֶּלָה. בָּרוּךְ אַתָּה, יְיָ, יוֹצֵר הַמְּאוֹרוֹת.

Blessing over wine:

בָּרוּךְ אַתָּה, יְיָ אֱלֹהֵינוּ, מֶלֶךְ הָעוֹלָם, בּוֹרֵא פְּרִי הַגָּפֶן.

150

If the wine service is included as part of the ceremony, a special cup should be used, one that has previously served a sacred place in the family or one obtained for the renewal service.

A Second Service

In the pamphlet *A Service of Christian Marriage,* published by Pantheon Press, two special services are outlined. One is for the anniversary of a marriage and the other, for a renewal of wedding vows. The order of the Service of Renewal is as follows.

Prelude, or special music chosen by husband and wife as particularly meaningful to them
Processional Hymn—*Now Thank We All Our God*
Greeting by Minister
Scripture Lesson(s) and Praise
Homily or Sermon on the Marriage
Renewal of Vows
Congregational Response
Intercessions
Declaration of Renewal
The Peace
Prayer of Thanksgiving or Holy Communion
Dismissal with Blessing
Recessional Hymn